QUESTIONS & ANSWERS:
Patent Law

QUESTIONS & ANSWERS:
Patent Law

Multiple Choice and Short Answer
Questions and Answers

By

Cynthia M. Ho
Clifford E. Vickrey Research Professor
Director, Intellectual Property & Technology Program
Loyola University Chicago School of Law

 LexisNexis®

ISBN#: 9780820570747

> **NOTE TO USERS**
> **To ensure that you are using the latest materials available in this area,
> please be sure to periodically check the LexisNexis Law School web site
> for downloadable updates and supplements at www.lexisnexis.com
> /lawschool**

Editorial Offices
744 Broad Street, Newark, NJ 07102 (973) 820-2000
201 Mission St., San Francisco, CA 94105-1831 (415) 908-3200
701 East Water Street, Charlottesville, VA 22902-7587 (434) 972-7600
www.lexis.com

(Pub.3225)

ABOUT THE AUTHOR

Cynthia M. Ho is the Clifford E. Vickrey Research Professor at Loyola Chicago School of Law, as well as the Director of Loyola's intellectual property program. Professor Ho has been a member of the faculty since 1997, where she teaches Intellectual Property, Patent Law, Comparative Patent Law, Policy and Health Care, as well as Civil Procedure. She is a recognized scholar of patent law who was been cited in several intellectual property and patent case books. In addition, she has served as a consultant to the United Nations Convention on Biological Diversity (CBD) on an issue at the interface of international patent law and biotechnology and has provided consultation to the National Institutes of Health (NIH). She has also provided lectures on patent law for the Bar/Bri Patent Bar Review.

Before joining the faculty at Loyola, Professor Ho practiced intellectual property with Fish & Neave (now the Fish & Neave IP group of Ropes & Gray). She participated in major litigation of high-technology cases involving patents, trade secrets, and unfair competition. In addition, as a registered member of the Patent Bar, she drafted and prosecuted patent applications.

PREFACE

This book may be useful for a variety of contexts, including supplementing a patent class, as well as the patent segment of an intellectual property class. In addition, although this book may be used to supplement study for the patent "bar," it is not intended to cover the same range of topics. In particular, the focus here is on substantive areas of patent law, rather than on the intricacies of patent examination that are important to the patent bar exam.

For those of you already familiar with the *Questions & Answers* series, you know that this book contains a variety of questions designed to test and reinforce your understanding. The questions vary in difficulty, ranging from identification of rules, to applying rules to specific fact patterns. For most topics, there are application examples to help test your understanding. In addition, for anyone who wishes to make the multiple choice questions even more challenging, you can try to answer the questions without looking at the options.

Although this book cannot possibly attempt to cover every aspect of patent law, hopefully it will at least provide a useful start to reinforcing your understanding through active learning. Perhaps some of the questions here will prompt you to create your own questions to challenge yourself and/or your classmates. After all, the best way to learn is to try to teach others — something that I am always striving to do.

I am grateful to LexisNexis for creating the *Questions & Answers* series, as well as for the opportunity to participate as an author.

Professor Cynthia M. Ho
Chicago, IL
November 12, 2007

TABLE OF CONTENTS

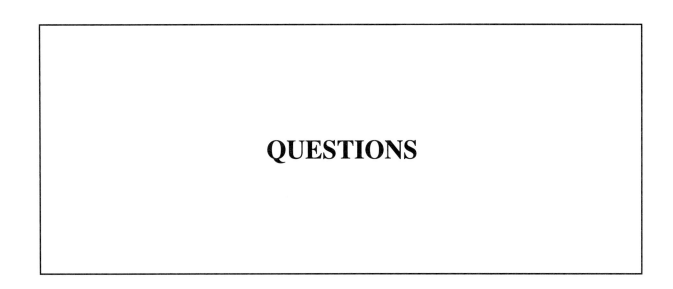

QUESTIONS

1. Which of the following is true concerning patentable subject matter:

   (A) To be patentable subject matter, an invention must constitute a process, machine, manufacture, or composition of matter.

   (B) The only relevant test for assessing patentable subject matter is whether the invention is man-made since "anything under the sun made by man" qualifies according to the Supreme Court.

   (C) New uses of previously known compositions are not patentable.

   (D) Improvements on previously known devices are not patentable.

2. Which of the following did the Supreme Court hold as patentable subject matter in *Diamond v. Chakrabarty?*

   (A) Observation of physical phenomena

   (B) Bacteria in their natural state

   (C) Methods of inoculating bacteria

   (D) Living organisms that have been genetically modified.

3. Which of the following is the most accurate statement concerning patentable subject matter?

   (A) Business methods are considered patentable subject matter despite the fact that the United States Supreme Court has never explicitly ruled on the subject.

   (B) Computer software is not patentable subject matter because it is subject to copyright protection.

   (C) A new algorithm is patentable subject matter, regardless of whether it is associated with a new product or process.

   (D) A new scientific principle concerning the universe would be patentable as a new discovery.

4. Which of the following is the most accurate statement concerning patentable subject matter?

   (A) Genetically modified plants may not be patentable under the Utility Patent Act because there is separate protection for plants under the Plant Variety Protection Act, as well as under the Plant Patent Act.

(B)   A method of performing surgery is not patentable subject matter because it would be immoral and unethical to prevent a surgeon from performing a medically necessary operation.

(C)   A peanut butter and jelly sandwich is patentable subject matter.

(D)   A patent applicant must affirmatively state which 101 category (i.e., composition of matter, etc.) the invention falls within in the application.

5.   How is a utility patent different than a design patent?

ANSWER:

6. Which of the following statements best describes the application of utility for inventions that relate to medicine?

    (A) A drug is useful if it is more efficacious than prior drugs.

    (B) A drug must satisfy FDA regulations for marketing of drugs in order to have utility.

    (C) A new medical device may be considered useful from a patent perspective, even if doctors do not think that it is an improvement over existing devices on the market.

    (D) All of the above are true.

7. Which of the following best describes the standard of utility?

    (A) The invention must be useful for a technical subject matter.

    (B) The invention must be functionally operable.

    (C) The invention must be operable for its intended purpose and not be immoral.

    (D) The invention must be functionally operable and have at least one specific, substantial and practical utility.

8. Which of the following inventions would have requisite utility under Section 101?

    (A) A painting that is recognized to have artistic value by those of skill in the art.

    (B) A painting that is useful in providing psychological benefits to those who see it because the color combinations are visually appealing.

    (C) A new toy for toddlers that is easier to hold and machine washable.

    (D) A sculpture that could be used as a door stop.

9. Which of the following inventions would have requisite utility under Section 101?

    (A) A perpetual motion invention, regardless of whether it can actually work in perpetuity because the idea is clearly useful.

    (B) A non-invasive method for minimizing wrinkles without injection, regardless of whether the application provides adequate evidence that the method works.

    (C) A machine that is capable of identifying the components of biological material, but is not useful for any purpose other than in a research setting.

    (D) A chemical composition that has no currently known utility, but is similar to another composition that is effective at inhibiting tumor growth.

[A] Applications

10. What is the distinction between a provisional and non-provisional application?

   (A) The provisional application lacks claims.

   (B) The provisional application may be filed free of charge.

   (C) A non-provisional application must contain drawings.

   (D) There is no distinction, other than a lower fee for provisional applications.

11. What is the significance of one year after a provisional application is filed?

   (A) The provisional application automatically converts to a non-provisional application.

   (B) The applicant may convert the provisional to a continuation application at this time.

   (C) The PTO will automatically examine the provisional application without any further action by the applicant.

   (D) The applicant must file a corresponding non-provisional application, or else lose the benefit of the filing date of the provisional application.

12. Which of the following is *false* about provisional applications?

   (A) The date of the provisional application may be relied upon by a corresponding non-provisional application filed within one year.

   (B) An applicant may properly mark a product that embodies the invention of a provisional application as "patented," since the application indicates that the applicant is seeking a patent.

   (C) A foreign patent application may use the priority date of a corresponding provisional application.

   (D) The PTO will not examine a provisional application.

13. When, if ever, are non-provisional patent applications published?

   (A) Never; only issued patents are published.

   (B) Approximately 18 months from the actual filing date.

   (C) Approximately 18 months from the earliest effective filing date.

   (D) Approximately 18 months from the earliest effective filing date for most non-provisional applications; never for provisional applications.

[B]   Claims

14.   Why are patent claims considered the most important part of a patent?

ANSWER:

15.   Which of the following describes what a claim must accomplish?

   (A)   Establish the utility of the invention over prior art.

   (B)   Describe how the invention is an improvement over the prior art.

   (C)   Describe how to make and use the invention.

   (D)   Describe the elements of the invention.

16.   Every valid claim has a preamble, transition phrase, and body, but the transition phrases, such as consisting or comprising, typically have a major impact on the scope of the claim. Why is the typically short transition word or phrase important and why would a drafter ever chose one over the other?

ANSWER:

17.   Which of the following is *not* true concerning the preamble to a claim?

   (A)   It is typically a short description of the claimed invention.

   (B)   There is no set minimum or maximum number of words required.

   (C)   It need not use any of the statutory classifications under 101.

   (D)   It is never relevant to construing the scope of the claim.

18.   When, if ever, would a preamble limit the scope of a claim?

ANSWER:

19.   Which of the following is most accurate concerning independent and dependent claims?

   (A)   A patent application must include both independent and dependent claims.

   (B)   A dependent claim refers to an independent claim and is only valid if the independent claim is valid.

   (C)   If an independent claim is valid, a dependent claim to the independent claim must also be valid.

(D) A dependent claim refers to an independent claim and includes all of the elements of the independent claim plus the elements cited in the dependent claim.

20. How does "claim differentiation" assist in claim construction?

ANSWER:

21. What happens if the USPTO rejects all the claims in its first communication (Office Action) with the patent owner?

(A) The applicant may respond to the office action and defend its claims, but may not amend the claims; this is the only opportunity the applicant will have to argue for patentability before the PTO either grants or denies a patent.

(B) The applicant may respond to the office action, including either defending and/or amending the claims; in addition, the applicant should be entitled to another opportunity.

(C) The applicant must elect to either respond to the office action, or appeal the result.

(D) The applicant must elect to either respond to the office action, or file a continuation application.

[A] General

22. What is the relevant time period for assessing whether claims satisfy the disclosure requirements of Section 112?

(A) The date of invention

(B) The date of application

(C) The date of examination by the PTO

(D) The date of infringement litigation

23. Can an applicant add additional information to the specification after the application is filed and rely upon the additional information to satisfy 112 requirements (assuming no continuation-in-part application)?

ANSWER:

24. Which of the following describes what an applicant may incorporate by reference in satisfying 112 disclosure requirements?

(A) Any written publication, including patents and articles

(B) Either a U.S. patent or a published U.S. application

(C) Any published patent

(D) A U.S. patent, published U.S. application, or a pending U.S. application

[B] Section 112 Disclosure — Enablement

25. Which of the following best describes whether a patent specification is enabling?

(A) It enables someone of skill in the art to make the invention.

(B) It enables someone of skill in the art to make and use the invention.

(C) It enables someone of skill in the art to make and use the invention by use of at least one working example.

(D) It enables any person to make and use the invention by clearly describing the scope of the invention.

26. If a patent application satisfies the written description requirement, does it necessarily satisfy the enablement requirement? Why or why not?

ANSWER:

27. To satisfy the enablement requirement, must all information necessary to make and use the claimed invention be included within the four corners of the application? Why or why not?

ANSWER:

28. What factors are relevant to assess whether "undue experimentation" would be necessary for a person of ordinary skill in the art to make or use the claimed invention?

ANSWER:

29. What does it mean that an area is "unpredictable" and how does that impact what must be disclosed according to 112?

ANSWER:

30. Can enablement be assessed without considering the claims? Why or why not?

ANSWER:

31. Can a rejection based on lack of enablement be corrected without introducing impermissible new matter? If so, how?

ANSWER:

32. Does enablement require an application to contain either working or prophetic examples?

ANSWER:

[C]   Section 112 Disclosure — Best Mode

33.   What is the "best mode" and how is it determined?

ANSWER:

34.   What is the policy behind the "best mode" requirement?

ANSWER:

35.   Which of the following best describes the best mode requirement?

   (A)   An applicant is required to disclose the best method of making the invention.

   (B)   An applicant is required to disclose the best method of using the invention.

   (C)   An applicant is required to disclose the best method of making and using the claimed invention.

   (D)   An applicant is required to disclose the best method of making and using the invention and is required to update the specification during the patent prosecution process if a better method is discovered.

[D]   Written Description

36.   What policy is served by the "written description" requirement?

ANSWER:

37.   Which of the following best describes when the "written description" requirement is satisfied?

   (A)   The patent application is in writing.

   (B)   The claims are based upon something that is written, as opposed to pictorial.

   (C)   The claims are supported by a specification that indicates the applicant was in possession of the claimed invention.

   (D)   The application contains a written description of the invention, concluding with one or more claims.

38.   If the PTO rejects a claim as lacking an adequate written description in the specification, which of the following best describes how the applicant can overcome the rejection?

(A) Amend the claim so that it is supported by the original specification.

(B) Amend the specification to provide adequate support for the claim.

(C) Submit an affidavit of the applicant that swears the applicant (and affiant) was in fact in possession of the claimed invention as of the filing date.

(D) Submit a published peer-reviewed paper authored by the applicant regarding the claimed invention as proof that the applicant was in possession of the claimed invention.

39. In which of the following instances would written description be at issue?

(A) An applicant claims the benefit of the filing date of an earlier application.

(B) An applicant introduces a new claim during prosecution.

(C) An originally filed claim is substantially amended during prosecution.

(D) All of the above.

[E] Section 112 ¶ 2 — Definiteness

40. What does 112, paragraph 2 require other than that a specification have at least one claim and what is the policy rationale for imposing such a requirement?

ANSWER:

41. Which of the following best describes whose perspective is relevant to assessing whether claims satisfy the definiteness requirement?

(A) Based upon the perspective of a lay jury, since this is a question of fact.

(B) Based upon the perspective of a person of skill in the art.

(C) Based upon the perspective of the judge, since patent claims are analogous to terms in a contract, which are routinely interpreted by judges.

(D) Based upon the inventor's perspective, as determined by an affidavit or deposition testimony.

42. Which of the following is true concerning the definiteness requirement?

(A) Vague or imprecise language such as the terms "substantially" and "about" is indefinite if not expressly explained in the specification.

(B) The technology of the claimed invention may be relevant in interpreting whether a claim is adequately definite.

(C) Extrinsic evidence may not be introduced to establish whether claims are definite.

(D) If the specification enables one of skill in the art to make and use the invention, the definiteness requirement is also established.

[F]   Section 112 ¶ 6 — Means Plus Function Claims

43. What is the fundamental difference between claims written in accordance with 112 paragraph 6 and all other claims?

ANSWER:

44. Which of the following states a limitation on means plus function claims?

(A) They are only applicable to mechanical inventions.

(B) Only one element of a claim may be expressed as a means plus function.

(C) Means plus function is not appropriate for a claim with a single element.

(D) The means plus function is interpreted such that the invention only includes the corresponding structure or element that is expressly disclosed in the specification.

45. How can a means plus function claim satisfy the definiteness requirement?

ANSWER:

[G]   Section 112 Disclosure — Examples

46. Joe develops a new method of making artificial skin. The method is described in detail in the patent application that concludes with one claim to the actual method. The application provides sufficient description such that one of skill in the art would be able to make the artificial skin. However, the application does not disclose that the process yields the most amount of artificial skin if Joe's trade secret compound is used as one of the starting materials. Which of the following best describes whether the application is consistent with disclosure requirements of 112?

(A) The application fails to disclose the best mode.

(B) The application fails to provide a written description of the invention, but the best mode is adequately disclosed.

(C) The application fails to satisfy the enablement requirement.

(D) The application satisfies the enablement requirement, but does not adequately disclose the best mode.

47. Abby invents a new type of artificial skin. The application describes in detail how to create the skin such that one of skill in the art would be able to make the claimed

invention and concludes with one claim to the artificial skin product. One of the starting materials is rubber, although rubber is only one of several components of the resulting artificial skin. Although any commercial-grade rubber will work, Abby actually uses her own rubber that she creates using a trade secret method that is much more inexpensive. Abby does not want to disclose her trade secret method in the application to maintain her competitive commercial advantage. However, Abby would prefer to disclose the brand name of her rubber over disclosing the entire method. Which of the following is true?

(A) Abby must disclose all steps to the method to comply with the best mode requirement.

(B) Abby need not disclose the steps to the method, but must at least disclose the brand name of her rubber.

(C) Whether or not Abby needs to disclose any information concerning her rubber depends on whether the rubber is considered a production element.

(D) Abby need not disclose any aspect of her process or the brand name since someone of skill in the art can make the claimed invention using any commercially available rubber.

FACTS FOR QUESTIONS 48-49:

Judy, a designer of shoes, comes up with a gel composition for running shoes that is sturdy and durable on the outside, yet provides cushioning. The ingredients are as follows:

65-85 A

15-20 B

10-15 C

Apparently, the composition does not work as intended when there is less than 65% A or more than 85% A. In addition, element A is part of a large class of 100 relatively new elements, called the fosse class. Judy has experimented with 55 members of the fosse class and found that about 20 of those members have similar properties to A. The remainder would not work for her invention.

48. Judy files a patent application with a claim as follows: "A composition for use in running shoes comprising 70% of an element of the fosse class, together with 20% B and 10%C." Which of the following is most accurate concerning whether her claim is consistent with 112?

(A) The claim is fully supported by the specification and should be allowed so long as it is consistent with 102 and 103.

(B) The claim should be rejected for lacking definiteness.

(C) The claim should be rejected for lack of enablement.

(D) The claim should be rejected for lacking definiteness and lack of written description.

49.   Judy has a second claim that reads as follows: A composition for use in running shoes comprising 10% A, 50% B, and 40% C. Which of the following is true?

   (A)   This claim satisfies definiteness, but lacks an adequate written description.

   (B)   The claim has an adequate written description, but is not enabled.

   (C)   The claim is enabled, but lacks a written description.

   (D)   The claim lacks an adequate written description and is also not enabled.

[A] General

50. Which of the following is most accurate concerning the application of section 102?

(A) A patent must issue if the invention satisfies any one of the criteria of 102(a)-(g).

(B) A patent must issue if none of the criteria of 102(a)-(g) exist.

(C) A patent cannot issue if any one of the criteria of 102(a)-(g) exist; but even if none of the criteria of 102(a)-(g) exists, a patent may still be denied.

(D) The applicant must explain why her invention is not barred by each section of 102 in her original patent application.

51. In comparing a claimed invention to a prior art reference under 102(a) or 102(b), which of the follow best describes what must be examined?

(A) Whether at least one element of the claimed invention is disclosed in the prior art reference.

(B) If the prior art reference is a patent, the claimed invention is compared to the claims of the prior art patent.

(C) If the prior art reference is a patent, the commercial embodiment of the prior art patent is compared to the claimed invention.

(D) Whether every element of the claimed invention is disclosed in the prior art reference.

[B] Date of Invention

52. For many provisions of 102, the date of invention is important. How is the "date of invention" established?

(A) The applicant must provide a date in the original application.

(B) The USPTO will use the filing date of the application as the presumptive date of invention; the applicant may later establish an earlier date by affidavit if the invention was actually reduced to practice before the filing date.

(C) The applicant must provide documentation to accompany the original application that shows the date of conception and reduction to practice of the invention.

(D) The USPTO will use the date provided by the applicant in the applicant's oath of invention, but that date may be later challenged by the USPTO.

53. If an applicant can establish a date of invention prior to the date of filing, how does this impact the analysis under 102?

   (A) The earlier date may be used to rebut rejections based on 102(a) and 102(b).

   (B) The earlier date may be used to rebut a rejection under 102(b).

   (C) The earlier date may be used to rebut a rejection under 102(a)

   (D) The earlier date is not relevant except for 102(g).

[C]   Section 102 Prior Art — Printed Publication

54. What constitutes a "printed publication" and what qualities must it have to constitute prior art?

ANSWER:

55. Which of the following best describes the test for determining whether a printed publication should be considered sufficiently accessible?

   (A) Whether the publication has been disseminated to the general public.

   (B) Whether the publication has been disseminated to the relevant public.

   (C) Whether the publication has been either distributed or indexed in a catalog.

   (D) Whether the reference has been made publicly accessible to the relevant public.

56. What factors were relevant to the Court's conclusion in *In re Klopfenstein* that the poster paper at an academic conference constituted a printed publication, even though it had not been reproduced, let alone distributed to the conference participants?

ANSWER:

57. Which of the following does *not* constitute a printed publication?

   (A) A description of all elements of an invention on an Internet blog.

   (B) A newspaper article describing all elements of the invention.

   (C) A single copy of a (Russian language) thesis describing all elements of the invention where the thesis is stored in a Russian library that is catalogued according to routine library practices, but not accessible on the Internet.

   (D) A single copy of an inventor's notebook that discloses all elements of an invention, where the notebook is kept in the attic of the inventor's summer house in Cape Cod, Massachusetts.

58. What is the difference — if any — regarding what constitutes a printed publication under 102(a) versus 102(b)?

ANSWER:

[D]   Section 102(a) — Anticipation

59. Can an applicant bar himself from a patent under 102(a)? Why or why not?

ANSWER:

60. Which of the following best describes a situation where an invention would be barred by 102(a)?

   (A)   The invention was disclosed in an article published in Ireland before the date of the applicant's invention.

   (B)   The invention was known or used anywhere in the world prior to the date of invention.

   (C)   The invention was on sale prior to the date of application.

   (D)   The invention was known in the United States before the date of the application.

61. Can a claimed invention be anticipated under 102(a) if the same invention was previously made by another, but not disclosed to the public?

ANSWER:

62. What must be disclosed in a prior art reference for it to be deemed anticipatory?

ANSWER:

63. Which of the following best describes the level of disclosure that an anticipatory reference would include?

   (A)   The reference must describe every element of the claimed invention, but need not disclose how to make the invention.

   (B)   The reference must describe every element of the claimed invention in adequate detail to enable a person of ordinary skill in the art to make the claimed invention without undue experimentation.

(C)   The reference must describe every element of the claimed invention in adequate detail to enable a person of ordinary skill in the art to make the claimed invention without undue experimentation and the reference must show utility of the disclosed invention.

(D)   The reference must disclose how to make the invention, although the reference need not disclose every element of the invention.

64.   An application describes compound ABC, as a newly created compound that alleviates migraines. The application has a single claim to ABC, without any limitation to its use. Assume prior art exists that describes ABC, including how to create ABC. However, the prior art does not describe or suggest that ABC may be useful for addressing migraines. Rather, the prior art merely describes compounds that have been created for further testing. Does the prior art anticipate the sole claim of ABC?

(A)   Yes.

(B)   No. Because the prior art did not identify ABC as pertinent to migraines, it does not anticipate.

(C)   No. Because the prior art did not describe how to use ABC for migraines, it does not anticipate.

(D)   Maybe. Although the prior art did not identify ABC as pertinent to migraines, if that would have been obvious to one of skill in the art, the claim is anticipated.

[E]   Inherency

65.   Which of the following best describes when a prior art reference anticipates an invention?

(A)   Every element of the claimed invention is disclosed in a single prior art reference.

(B)   Every element of the claimed invention is expressly disclosed in a single prior art reference.

(C)   Every element of the claimed invention is disclosed expressly or inherently in a claimed invention.

(D)   Every element of the claimed invention is disclosed inherently in a claimed invention.

66.   Which of the following best describes how an element may be deemed inherent in a prior art reference such that an invention is anticipated even though the reference does not expressly disclose each element?

(A)   Extrinsic evidence must establish that a person of skill in the art appreciated or recognized the inherent aspect at the earlier making of the prior art invention.

(B)   Extrinsic evidence must establish that the inherent element would be likely to exist.

(C) Extrinsic evidence must establish that the inherent element would exist as a natural result of the prior art invention, regardless of whether that result was appreciated at the time by those of skill in the art.

(D) Extrinsic evidence must show that the inherent element would likely exist and that a person of skill in the art appreciated or recognized the inherent aspect.

[F] Genus/Species

67. Which of the following is true about anticipation under 102(a)?

(A) A prior art species anticipates a claimed genus.

(B) A prior art genus anticipates a claimed species

(C) Genus-species anticipation issues are only relevant to chemical and biological inventions

(D) An invention may be anticipated if it is either a genus or species relative to prior art.

68. An application claims a sole which touches the bottom of the foot, where the sole is connected to at least one other item that touches the foot. Prior art discloses sandals and sneakers, both of which may be worn on the feet. Which of the following is true?

(A) The claim is anticipated by either the sandals or the sneakers alone.

(B) The claim is anticipated by considering the sandal and sneaker prior art in combination.

(C) The claim is not anticipated by either the sandals or the sneakers since neither discloses every element of the claim.

(D) The claim is not anticipated by either the sandals or the sneakers even if they disclose every element of the claim if one of skill in the art would not be able to make all inventions within the scope of the claim.

69. An application claims a chemical composition having 5-10% A and 95-90% B. Which of the following prior art references would anticipate this claim?

(A) Prior art composition containing 8% A and 92% B

(B) Prior art composition containing 2% A and 98% B

(C) Prior art composition containing 1-4% A and 99-96% B.

(D) Prior art composition containing 12% A and 82% B

[G] Section 102(a) vs. Section 102(b)

70. Which of the following best describes the critical date of reference for 102(a) versus 102(b); in other words, what is the relevant date used to compare a claimed invention with prior art?

(A)   Both provisions use the date of invention.

(B)   Both provisions use the date of application.

(C)   The critical date for 102(a) is the date of invention whereas the date for 102(b) is more than one year prior to the date of application.

(D)   The critical date for 102(a) is the date of application whereas the date for 102(b) is more than one year prior to the date of application.

71.   Which of the following best describes a distinction between 102(a) versus 102(b)?

(A)   102(a) refers to situations that occur before the applicant's filing date whereas 102(b) refers to situations that occur more than one year before the applicant's filing date.

(B)   102(a) refers to situations that occur before the applicant's filing date whereas 102(b) refers to situations that occur more than one year before the applicant's date of invention.

(C)   102(a) refers to activity conducted solely by persons other than the applicant whereas 102(b) refers to patent-barring activity conducted solely by the applicant.

(D)   102(a) refers to activity conducted solely by persons other than the applicant, whereas 102(b) refers to activity by any person, including the applicant, if it occurs more than one year before the date of application.

[H]   Section 102(b) — Statutory Bar

72.   What policy is fostered by 102(b)? In particular, if an applicant is truly the first to invent, why should she be barred from a patent?

ANSWER:

73.   Whose actions may result in barring a patent under 102(b)?

(A)   The inventor/applicant only

(B)   Any person, including, but not limited to the inventor/applicant

(C)   Only someone besides the inventor/applicant

(D)   The inventor/applicant or her patent attorney

74.   Can an applicant be denied a patent based upon public use of an invention by a third party more than one year before the date of application of the patent?

(A)   Yes; this would constitute a statutory bar.

(B)   No; although the same activity by an inventor would foreclose the right to a patent, the use by a third party does not disqualify patentability.

    (C)   No; use of a claimed invention by a third party would be experimental use.

    (D)   Maybe; whether a patent is barred depends on the extent to which the third party's use was within the control of the applicant.

75. Which of the following does *not* describe a situation where an applicant of a novel invention will lose the right to obtain a patent?

    (A)   The invention was described in a printed publication located in Germany more than one year before the date of the application.

    (B)   The invention was described in a U.S. patent issued more than one year before the date of the application.

    (C)   The invention was sold by the applicant in the U.S. more than one year before the date of the application

    (D)   The invention was used in a foreign country more than one year before the date of the application.

[I]   Section 102(b) — Public Use

76. What constitutes "public use" under 102(b)?

ANSWER:

77. Which of the following best describes a situation where an invention is in public use under 102(b), assuming the use occurs more than one year before the date of the application?

    (A)   The invention is used by at least one member of the relevant public.

    (B)   The invention is used by a single person without restriction, even if the person does not fully appreciate the invention.

    (C)   The invention is used by a single person without restriction, but only if the person is a person of skill in the relevant art.

    (D)   The invention could have been used by any person of skill in the prior art, regardless of whether the invention was actually used.

78. Fred invents a device that enables him to strap a child seat to rolling luggage safely, thereby freeing up one of his hands to carry another piece of luggage. He was prompted to create this invention out of his own needs in traveling with his infant son. Once he discovers how useful it is, he distributes twenty devices to his family and friends. He does not ask for any money, but does tell them to let him know what they think about his invention so that he can perfect it before approaching someone to make it in commercial quantities. Two years after distributing his device, he files a patent

application, claiming the device that he provided to his friends and family without any changes. Which of the following is most accurate concerning whether Fred will be able to obtain a patent?

(A)   Fred will be barred a patent based solely on his own public use.

(B)   Although Fred's device was in public use more than one year before the application was filed, he is not barred under 102(b) because he did not seek payment for his device.

(C)   Although Fred's device was in public use more than one year before the application was filed, he is not barred under 102(b) because he asked for input from friends and family.

(D)   Fred will be barred a patent based upon public use under 102(b) because the devices embodying his invention were not within his control and he was not testing the claimed invention.

79.   Wygan, a pharmaceutical company, has a patent on a chemical composition. Wygan sells the composition commercially for heart disease. The product is a big success and sells broadly. Near the end of the patent term, Wygan discovers that the composition also cures indigestion. Wygan files a patent application claiming a method of using the composition to cure indigestion within six months of its discovery. Is Wygan entitled to a patent?

(A)   No, the new claim is anticipated.

(B)   No, the new claim is barred because the underlying composition has been in public use.

(C)   Yes, although the composition is not new, the claim is directed to a method of using the composition and that method is not in public use for more than one year before the application.

(D)   Yes, although Wygan did some testing, the public use will not bar Wygan from a patent because it constitutes experimental use.

80.   Barney develops a new method of making beer. He does not tell anyone about his method, although he does sell his own beer at his bar in Boston, Massachusetts. The method of making the beer is not apparent from the beer itself. Sarah independently invents the same method for making beer two years after Barney first sells his beer. Sarah files a patent application claiming both the method of making beer, as well as the beer itself. Which of the following best describes whether Sarah is precluded from obtaining a patent?

(A)   Yes. Barney's prior public use bars Sarah's claims for both the method of making the beer, as well as the beer itself.

(B)   No. Barney's activity does not bar Sarah from obtaining a patent because only a patentee's own activity is relevant under 102(b).

    (C)   Partially — Barney's prior sales constitute a 102(b) bar to the beer claims, but not the method claims.

    (D)   Partially — Barney's prior sales constitute a 102(b) bar to the method claims, but not the beer claims.

[J] Section 102(b) — On Sale Bar

81.   What types of activities are encompassed by the "on sale" bar provision of 102(b)?

    (A)   Actual sale of the claimed invention.

    (B)   Assignment of the patent.

    (C)   Actual sale or offer to sell the claimed invention.

    (D)   Actual sale or offer to sell the claimed invention; in addition, assignment of the patent rights.

82.   How does a court assess whether a claimed invention is deemed "on sale"?

ANSWER:

83.   Maggie invents and reduces to practice a new and nonobvious sports bottle. She makes an offer to sell fifty boxes of her bottles to the Discount Store, which is accepted. However, the Discount Store goes out of business without having paid for the bottles. Subsequently, Maggie gets discouraged and does not attempt to make any further sales. Which of the following best describes whether Maggie will be subject to the on sale bar and when that bar would be calculated from?

    (A)   Maggie's offer to sell to Discount Store triggers the on sale bar; she has one year from the date of that offer to file her application or else be barred from a patent.

    (B)   The acceptance of the offer by Discount Store triggers the on sale bar; Maggie has one year from the date of that acceptance to file her application or else be barred from a patent.

    (C)   Maggie's invention has never been on sale because she never actually completed a sale.

    (D)   Maggie's invention was never on sale because it was not ready for patenting.

84.   Maggie is a manufacturer and supplier of all types of bottles. She offers to sell a sports bottle top that can be placed on any standard can of soda pop to enable a user to drink from the can without spilling. At the time she makes the offer, she has not yet figured out how to make this top, although she knows that is her end goal. Her offer is accepted. Thereafter, Maggie actually reduces the invention to practice and ships the relevant bottle tops. At what point — if any — is her invention on sale?

(A)   At the time she made the offer.

(B)   At the time the offer was accepted.

(C)   At the time she delivered the tops.

(D)   Never — her invention was never on sale because it was not ready for patenting at the time her offer was made.

[K]   Section 102(b) and the Relevance of Experimental Use

85.   What is "experimental use" and how is it relevant to analysis of patentability under 102?

ANSWER:

86.   In which of the following situations may experimental use negate an act that would otherwise bar patentability?

(A)   Public use under 102(b) only

(B)   Public use or sale of an invention under 102(b)

(C)   Sale or offer of sale of an invention under 102(b)

(D)   An anticipatory prior public use under 102(a)

87.   Which of the following is true?

(A)   If a court finds that there was experimental use of the claimed invention, then the defendant can establish that there was experimental use that negates the defendant's infringing activity.

(B)   The experimental use defense can negate any public use of an invention that occurs prior to the filing date.

(C)   The experimental use defense can only negate public use that is less than one year before the filing date of an application.

(D)   An applicant can overcome a statutory on-sale bar if experimental use is established.

[L]   Section 102(c) — Abandonment

88.   What does "abandonment" mean under 102(c)?

(A)   Abandonment of the right to use the invention.

(B)   Abandonment of the right to obtain a patent.

(C)   Abandonment of the right to use an invention, as well as the right to obtain a patent.

(D) Abandonment of the right to enforce a patent.

[M] Section 102(d) — Foreign Filing Bar

89. What policy is effectuated by 102(d)?

ANSWER:

90. When may a patent be barred under 102(d)?

(A) When the same invention was first patented in a foreign country by the same inventor, regardless of when the foreign or U.S. application was filed.

(B) When the same invention was first patented in a foreign country and the U.S. application was filed more than twelve months after the corresponding foreign application.

(C) When the same invention was claimed in a foreign application filed more than twelve months before the U.S. application.

(D) When the inventor uses a claimed invention in public outside the United States more than a year before the U.S. filing.

91. Which of the following is *not* an invention "first patented" in a foreign country pursuant to 102(d)?

(A) If it is disclosed in a published patent application.

(B) If it is subject to a patent-like exclusionary grant, even if the no examination is required prior to the grant.

(C) Invention has been allowed by a foreign patent office.

(D) Invention has been provided a foreign patent, albeit with only a seven-year term.

92. Will a patent be denied in the U.S. if a corresponding foreign patent has issued based upon a foreign application filed more than twelve months before a U.S. application?

(A) No.

(B) Yes, regardless of who filed the foreign application.

(C) Yes, but only if the foreign application is filed by the inventor.

(D) Yes, if the foreign application is filed by the inventor or by the assignee of the inventor.

93. An application disclosing compounds A, B, and C is filed in Germany, claiming only compound C. An identical application is filed in the U.S. by the same inventor, but with claims to A and B, as well as C. Which of the following is true?

(A)   The U.S. application is barred under 102(a) regardless of when the German application was filed.

(B)   The U.S. application is barred under 102(b) if the German application was filed more than one year before the U.S. application.

(C)   The U.S. application is barred under 102(d) if a German patent issues.

(D)   The U.S. application will issue as a patent (assuming not obvious), at least for claims to A and B because those were not present in the German application.

94.   If an application for a patent is filed in Hungary for subject matter that is statutorily impermissible in Hungary, what is the impact of such an application on the identical subject matter later subject to an application in the U.S.?

(A)   The Hungarian application has no bearing on the U.S. application under 102 since the Hungarian application is not valid.

(B)   The Hungarian application would bar a U.S. patent for the same invention if the U.S. application is filed more than one year after the Hungarian application.

(C)   The Hungarian application will not bar a U.S. patent unless it is published more than one year before the U.S. application.

(D)   The Hungarian application will not bar a U.S. patent so long as there is one common inventor because the U.S. application can claim the benefit of the earlier filing date.

[N]   Section 102(e) — Secret Prior Art from an Earlier-Filed Application

95.   What does 102(e)(1) prohibit from patenting and how is that relevant to the policy of granting patents to the person who is "first to invent"?

ANSWER:

96.   What is the effective date of a 102(e) prior art reference?

(A)   The date of conception of the invention.

(B)   The filing date.

(C)   The publication date

(D)   The date of issuance of the prior art patent.

97.   Which of the following is true about 102(e)(1)?

(A)   An applicant can be denied a patent under 102(e)(1) if a prior U.S. patent application claimed the identical invention.

(B)   An applicant can be denied a patent under 102(e)(1) if a prior U.S. patent application described the applicant's invention, but only if the prior application issues as a U.S. patent.

(C)   An applicant can be denied a patent under 102(e)(1) if a prior published U.S. patent application was filed before the applicant's invention, regardless of whether applicant had any actual knowledge of the earlier invention.

(D)   An applicant can be denied a patent under 102(e)(1) if a prior published U.S. patent application was filed before the applicant.

98.   Which of the following is true about 102(e)(2)?

(A)   An applicant can be denied a patent if the invention was previously claimed in a U.S. patent filed by another.

(B)   An applicant can be denied a patent if the invention was previously described in a U.S. patent before the applicant's date of invention.

(C)   An applicant can be denied a patent if the invention was previously described in any PCT application filed by another before the applicant's date of invention.

(D)   An applicant can be denied a patent if the invention was previously claimed in a PCT application filed by another.

99.   George develops a new windshield wiper on July 15, 2006. Kitty, a Canadian citizen, separately develops a windshield wiper and files a U.S. patent application. Her application publishes on June 1, 2006. George thereafter files a U.S. patent application. George's claimed windshield wiper is described, although not claimed, in Kitty's published application. Which of the following is true?

(A)   Kitty's application is a complete bar to George under 102(e).

(B)   Kitty's application will not bar George from obtaining a patent unless and until Kitty is granted a patent.

(C)   Kitty's application will not bar George from obtaining a patent because only applications filed by U.S. nationals are a bar under 102(e)(1).

(D)   Kitty's application will not bar George from obtaining a patent because she only describes, but does not claim George's invention.

100.   Edna develops a mechanical means for turning pages using a foot pedal. She timely files a patent application to ensure that she does not bar herself from obtaining a patent. Edna broadly claims her invention to cover a variety of means for turning pages using a foot pedal. Before Edna files her application, Kristen had previously filed an application. Kristen's application has claims directed to a different type of page-turner, but the specification describes a variety of mechanisms to turn pages, including a foot pedal, such that all elements of Edna's claim are disclosed. Edna was not aware of Kristen's application because Kristen's application did not publish until after Edna filed her application. Which of the following is true?

(A)   Kristen's application is not prior art because Edna could not have had any actual knowledge of the application.

(B)   Kristen's application is not prior art because it did not become public until after Edna filed her application.

(C)   Kristen's application constitutes a complete bar to Edna's claim.

(D)   Kristen's application will not bar Edna from obtaining a patent because Kristen's claims differ from Edna's.

[O]   Section 102(f) — Derivation

101.   What does 102(f) bar that is not already addressed by another provision of 102?

ANSWER:

102.   Vicki reads an article in *Health* magazine that a new compound has anti-inflammatory properties and is subject to testing for dermatitis. Vicki, who is a chemist, thinks that this is interesting and that something with anti-inflammatory properties may be useful for other purposes as well. In particular, she uses the compound, with some modifications and additional elements, to create a topical treatment for chickenpox that reduces inflammation, as well as itching. She admits that she was inspired by the *Health* magazine article and was not aware of the compound previously, but believes that she is nonetheless entitled to a patent. Is she barred by 102(f)?

ANSWER:

103.   Apple sues Britney for infringing her patent that claims genetically modified rice. Apple's complaint alleges that Britney infringes based on the fact that rice grown by her is covered by the claims of Apple's patent. Britney would like to challenge the patent. After extensive investigation, she has discovered that Apple's purported invention is based on information that Apple was told by a farmer when she visited India. Although the Indian rice disclosed to Apple was not genetically modified, it had the same properties as what Apple claims. Which of the following most accurately describes a basis upon which Britney can successfully challenge Apple's patent?

(A)   Section 102(a), since Apple's invention was previously known.

(B)   Section 102(b), if Apple's patent application was filed more than a year after her trip to India.

(C)   Section 102(f).

(D)   Section 102(e).

[P]   Section 102(g)

104.   What is the difference between 102(g)(1) and 102(g)(2)

(A)   Both provisions address interference proceedings, but only 102(g)(1) allows for evidence of invention outside the United States.

(B)   Both provisions address interference proceedings, but only 102(g)(2) permits the inventor first to conceive to possibly be awarded a patent through reasonable diligence.

(C)   102(g)(1) bars patents in interference proceedings, whereas 102(g)(2) bars patent in non-interference contexts.

(D)   102(g)(1) bars patents in non-interference context and 102(g)(2) bars patents in interference proceedings.

105.   What is the difference between conception and reduction to practice?

ANSWER:

106.   What is "diligence" and when is it relevant in assessing who should obtain a patent?

ANSWER:

107.   Why is "reasonable diligence" not applicable where an inventor is both first to conceive and first to reduce to practice?

ANSWER:

108.   In which of the following situations would "reasonable diligence" be relevant?

(A)   In an interference proceeding, Inventor A is first to conceive and first to reduce to practice.

(B)   In an interference proceeding, Inventor B is first to conceive, but last to reduce to practice.

(C)   In a patent infringement proceeding, defendant establishes that third party X made an invention in a WTO country prior to the (plaintiff) patentee and did not abandon, suppress, or conceal the invention.

(D)   In a patent infringement proceeding, defendant establishes that third party X made the invention in the United States prior to the plaintiff (patentee) and did not abandon, suppress, or conceal the invention.

(E)   Choices B and D are correct.

109.   What is "corroboration" for purposes of 102(g) and how is it established?
ANSWER:

110.   Which of the following best describes whose actions are relevant in assessing whether an invention has been abandoned, suppressed, or concealed?

(A)   Only the inventor.

(B)   The inventor, as well as *any* corporate assignee.

(C)   Only the assignee.

(D)   The inventor, as well as any corporate assignee, including the actions of the patent department.

111.   Which of the following is true concerning concealment of an invention?

(A)   An invention may be deemed concealed because of unreasonable delay between reduction to practice and filing.

(B)   A long passage of time between reduction to practice and filing of an application establishes concealment.

(C)   If an invention is not filed due to delay of a corporate patent department, that delay is not imputed to the inventor.

(D)   An inference of concealment may be rebutted if the inventor/applicant is working on a commercial model of the invention.

[Q]   Section 102(g)(2)

112.   Which of the following does *not* describe a situation in which 102(g)(2) is applicable?

(A)   In ex parte prosecution of a patent application to assess whether an applicant is barred by an earlier invention.

(B)   In federal court litigation if a defendant challenges a patent based upon this section.

(C)   In inter partes prosecution of a patent application between competing applicants to assess who is the first true inventor.

(D)   All of the above.

113.   Which of the following describes a situation where an applicant will be barred a patent based upon 102(g)(2)?

(A)   The inventor previously disclosed the invention, such that it is deemed abandoned, suppressed, or concealed.

(B)   The invention was first made by another, anywhere in the world.

(C)   The invention was first made by another in the United States by someone who had not abandoned, suppressed, or concealed.

(D)   The invention was first made by another in any WTO country by someone who had not abandoned, suppressed, or concealed.

[R]   Interference

114.   What is the goal of an interference proceeding and why is it not relevant in countries that operate under a "first to file" system?

ANSWER:

115.   Which of the following best describes interferences?

(A)   An interference is a proceeding in which a district court assesses which party was first to invent.

(B)   An interference is an adjudicatory proceeding in which the USPTO determines which party was first to invent.

(C)   Every patent application is subject to an interference proceeding to assess whether the inventor was the first to invent, and thus entitled to a patent.

(D)   An interference is an adjudicatory proceeding in which the USPTO determines which party was first to invent; however, an interference may only be declared between applicants that are U.S. residents since proof of inventive activity must occur within the United States.

116.   Which of the following describes a situation where an interference may *not* be declared?

(A)   Two patents with differing claims, but overlapping subject matter within the claims.

(B)   A patent and a patent application with differing claims, but overlapping subject matter in at least one claim.

(C)   Two patent applications with differing claims, but overlapping subject matter.

(D)   Two patent applications with identical claims.

117. What policy goal is fostered by denying patents for inventions which are not anticipated by a single reference, but are nonetheless obvious to a person of ordinary skill in the art?

ANSWER:

118. Can an invention be obvious where it would have been obvious to *try,* even if not previously accomplished?

ANSWER:

119. Which of the following provides the most accurate description of the test for evaluating whether an invention is obvious?

   (A)   The invention shows a flash of genius.

   (B)   The invention is distinguishable from the prior art in that it would require more than the work of a skilled mechanic.

   (C)   The invention is obvious based on a consideration of the scope and content of the prior art, the level of ordinary skill in the relevant art, and the differences between the prior art and the claimed invention.

   (D)   All of the above are true.

120. What types of prior art references under 102 — if any — can be used to evaluate whether an invention is obvious under 103?

ANSWER:

121. Is there a minimum or maximum number of prior art references that may be considered in evaluating whether an invention is obvious under 103?

ANSWER:

122. How many prior art references may an obviousness rejection be based on?

   (A) Obviousness must be based upon at least two prior art references.

   (B) A claim may be properly considered obvious over a single reference if that reference discloses every element of the claim.

   (C) A claim may be considered obvious over a single reference even if the reference does not disclose every element of the claim if there is a teaching, motivation, or suggestion to modify the prior art reference to achieve all elements of the claim.

   (D) Obviousness may be based upon two prior art references if the two references together contain all the elements of the claimed invention without regard to the nature of the references, including whether they would have been pertinent to the problem being solved.

123. Can an invention be deemed obvious over prior art references that the inventor had no actual knowledge of?

ANSWER:

124. Can an invention be found to be obvious based upon prior art that is from a different technological endeavor? Why or why not?

ANSWER:

125. Which of the following best describes the distinction between relevant prior art for the purpose of evaluating nonobviousness under 103 versus relevant prior art for assessing novelty under 102?

   (A) The identical prior art is used for purposes of 102 and 103; the only distinction is that more references may be utilized for 103.

   (B) Prior art under 102 is limited to art that a person of ordinary skill would be expected to have knowledge of, whereas relevant prior art for 103 is limited to art within the relevant field of endeavor.

   (C) Prior art under 103 is limited to art within the same field of technology, or art that is pertinent to the problem being solved, whereas art in any field of technology may be utilized for 102.

   (D) Prior art under 102 includes any field of technology, even if not related to the problem to be solved, whereas prior art for evaluating 103 must be limited to what the inventor had actual knowledge of.

126. What is the relevant time period for comparing the scope and content of prior art with the claimed invention?

(A) The date of invention.

(B) The date of application — if later than the date of invention.

(C) The date the patent issues.

(D) The date the patent is enforced in an infringement suit.

127. Donna files a patent application on a flexible can-cooling sleeve that conforms to the shape of a can, using material X, to keep it cold. Would the prior use of insulated foam cup holders constitute prior art that could be used to bar Donna's patent, even if Donna's claim specifies the use of a material other than foam?

ANSWER:

128. Donna files a patent application on a flexible can-cooling sleeve that conforms to the shape of a can using material X that can be placed around a can of soda pop to keep it cold. Which of the following would be most likely to present a problem for Donna under 103?

(A) Donna's friend Eva had previously told her that someone should invent a way to keep soda cans cool since this is a problem that not only bothers Eva, but many of Eva's friends. In addition, Eva suggested that having something that easily wraps around the can would be a good idea, although Eva did not suggest any specific types of material.

(B) A patent application filed before Donna's discloses a bag for keeping food cold on picnics using material X; the patent was filed before Donna's application, but has not yet been published.

(C) A Venezuelan patent is granted on an application filed before Donna's conception that discloses a circular ice pack that conforms to the wearer's body. The patent issues after Donna files her application. In addition, neither the application nor patent were in English.

(D) A patent issued before Donna's application that describes a heating pad to place under a cup of coffee to keep the coffee warm.

129. What factors are considered in assessing who is the person of relevant skill in the art with respect to 103 obviousness and must every factor be present in all cases?

ANSWER:

130. What is the TSM test, otherwise known as a "teaching, suggestion, or motivation" to modify or combine references and how is it to be applied?

ANSWER:

131. Barry has an idea for a new way to get around on wheels and seeks a patent on his invention. Although there is nothing identical to Barry's invention that exists in the prior art, all elements of Barry's invention do exist in the analogous art, including the number of wheels, as well as the type of motor used to operate the device. However, none of the prior art expressly suggests combining all of Barry's claimed elements. Explain whether Barry's invention is obviousness and be sure to address what factors are relevant, including any that are important, but not expressly noted in these facts.

ANSWER:

132. What are secondary considerations and how are they used in an analysis of 103 obviousness?

ANSWER:

133. Which of the following best describes how secondary considerations are to be utilized in an obviousness consideration?

(A) If a majority of secondary considerations exist, an invention is nonobvious.

(B) Only secondary considerations that have a nexus to the claimed invention may be considered, but there is no set number that must exist to establish an invention as nonobvious.

(C) If a majority of secondary considerations exist, there is no need to consider the difference between the claimed invention and the prior art.

(D) Secondary considerations should be analyzed first because they constitute objective indicia that guard against hindsight analysis.

134. Why might commercial success or widespread licensing not have an appropriate nexus to the claimed invention?

ANSWER:

135. Which of the following secondary considerations would best suggest that a patented glow-in-the-dark yo-yo was nonobvious?

(A)   The patentee's yo-yo sells well and is licensed by others, despite the fact that the patentee has no prior sales or licensing experience.

(B)   The yo-yo is one of the most coveted toys of the Christmas season.

(C)   The patent owner has licensed the patents to many others.

(D)   All of the above are true.

136. When, if ever, will subject matter developed by another that constitutes prior art under 102(e), (f), or (g) not bar a patent based upon obviousness?

ANSWER:

[A] General

137. Which of the following best describes what it means to be entitled to an earlier filing date under the current patent act?

(A) The application is assumed to have been filed at the earlier date with respect to its priority in the queue for prosecution at the USPTO, but not for purposes of calculating the patent term.

(B) The application is assumed to have been filed at the earlier date with respect to its priority in the queue for prosecution at the USPTO, as well as for purposes of calculating the patent terms

(C) The application is given the earlier filing date as the date of invention for purposes of prior art evaluation, but not for purposes of calculating the patent term.

(D) The application is given the earlier filing date as the date of invention for purposes of prior art evaluation, as well as for purposes of calculating the patent term.

138. What requirement in both sections 119 and 120 of the Patent Act ensure that an applicant is fairly entitled to claim an earlier filing date for purposes of prior art than the actual filing date?

ANSWER:

[B] Earlier Effective Date — U.S. Application (Section 120)

139. Which of the following is *not* required for an application to be entitled to the benefit of the filing date of an earlier U.S. application?

(A) At least one inventor in common between the two applications.

(B) Co-pending applications at the time the second application is filed.

(C) A reference to the earlier filed application in the second application.

(D) At least one assignee in common between the two applications.

140. In which of the following situations would the applications be considered "co-pending" for purposes of claiming an earlier effective filing date?

(A) The first application is issued as a patent before the second application is filed.

(B)   The first application is abandoned after the second application is filed.

(C)   The first application is abandoned before the second application is filed.

(D)   None of the above.

141.   Joe files a patent application on September 1, 2007. The application asserts that it is a continuation of an application that Joe and Jeff filed on December 1, 2006, and as such, it claims the benefit of the earlier filing date. The two applications share the same specification, but the claims are not the same. At the present time, the earlier application (by Joe and Jeff) is still pending. Which of the following is true?

(A)   The PTO will use December 1, 2006 as the date of invention with respect to prior art for all claims because the specifications are identical.

(B)   The PTO will use September 1, 2007 as the date of invention with respect to prior art for all claims that are supported by the first application.

(C)   The PTO will use the December 1, 2006 as the date of invention with respect to prior art for all claims that are supported by the first application.

(D)   The PTO will use September 1, 2007 as the date of invention, since the inventors are not identical.

142.   Assume that a patent application is filed September 1, 2007. An article was published on August 9, 2007 that completely described every element of the claimed invention in the application, as well as how to make and use the invention. Can an applicant overcome a rejection of anticipation based upon the article?

(A)   No; this situation fits 102(a) anticipation, so no patent may issue.

(B)   No; the invention is barred by 102(b), so no patent may issue.

(C)   Maybe; the applicant may overcome an anticipation rejection only if there is proof that the claimed invention was completed before August 9, 2007.

(D)   Maybe; the applicant may overcome an anticipation rejection if the application is entitled to benefit of an earlier filing date from an earlier application — before August 9, 2007 — such that intervening prior art would not be counted against the applicant.

143.   Jill files a patent application on January 2, 2006, that disclosed a bouncy ball made of compound X. The application does not disclose any other compound useful for the invention. This application has one claim, which states:

I claim a ball made from X.

Jill later discovers that any material solid at room temperature works fine for her ball. On September 15, 2007, Jill files a CIP application that is identical to the parent application of January 2, 2006, except Jill adds new information to the specification concerning how to make and use balls made of other solid materials, including plastic,

EARLIER EFFECTIVE FILING DATES

rubber, and foam. In addition, the CIP makes a specific reference to the earlier application and asserts entitlement to that date. The claims in the new application are as follows:

1. A ball made of solid material.

2. The ball of claim 1 wherein the solid material is X.

During examination of the CIP, the PTO discovers a publication that was publicly available on August 1, 2007 that discloses balls made of solid material. Which of the following is true?

(A)   All claims of Jill's CIP application are anticipated by the publication.

(B)   Both claims of Jill's CIP application are valid over the publication because they are entitled to the January 2, 2006 filing date.

(C)   The first claim of Jill's CIP application is anticipated, but the second claim is valid over the publication.

(D)   The first claim of Jill's CIP application is valid over the publication, but the second claim is anticipated.

[C]   Earlier Effective Filing Date — Foreign Application (Section 119)

144.   Which of the following best describes what type of U.S. patent applications are entitled to the benefit of an earlier filing date under Section 119 of the Patent Act?

(A)   Applications from non-U.S. citizens.

(B)   Applications claiming a priority date from applications filed anywhere outside the U.S.

(C)   Applications claiming a priority date from applications not filed in the U.S., but filed in a country that allows priority claims to U.S. applications or is a WTO member country.

(D)   All of the above.

145.   Which of the following accurately states a requirement for an application to claim an earlier filing date under 119?

(A)   The parent application must be copending.

(B)   The second application must be filed within twelve months from the earliest foreign application.

(C)   The second application must be filed within twelve months from the latest foreign application.

(D)   The second application must be filed by an individual who applied for the foreign application.

146. Claudia, a citizen of Spain, files an application in Spain on February 2, 2005 for a time travel machine. She files a continuation application in Spain on October 1, 2006. Claudia files a U.S. application on September 1, 2007 that has the identical disclosure as the October 1, 2006 application. Can Claudia claim the benefit of an earlier filing date and if so, which date?

(A) No, Claudia cannot claim the benefit of an earlier filing date because she is not a U.S. citizen.

(B) Yes, Claudia can claim the benefit of October 1, 2006 since her U.S. application is filed within twelve months of that date.

(C) No, Claudia cannot claim the benefit of an earlier filing date since it is more than twelve months since her earliest foreign filing date.

(D) Yes, Claudia can claim the benefit of February 2, 2005 as the priority date since that is the earliest filing date and she has filed a U.S. application within twelve months of her latest relevant foreign application.

FACTS FOR QUESTIONS 147-49:

Frank files a patent application with the Japanese Patent Office on March 12, 2006; Japan is a WTO member country. The application describes a toothbrush with novel fibers that are especially good at combating bacteria and plaque. In addition, the application describes a new shape for the bristles that is designed to improve plaque removal. The sole claim of the Japanese application relates to the novel fibers.

147. Frank files an application with the USPTO on March 1, 2007 with the identical claim as the Japanese application (except in English). Which of the following is most accurate?

(A) Frank will be denied a patent because the prior application constitutes a bar under 102(a).

(B) Frank will be denied a patent under 102(b), but only if the Japanese application has been published.

(C) Frank will be denied a patent under 102(b), but only if the Japanese patent application was not co-pending at the time of the U.S. filing.

(D) Frank will not be barred by either 102(a) or 102(b), even if the Japanese application has been published.

148. For this question, assume that Frank files a U.S. application with an identical disclosure to the March 1, 2007 Japanese application, except that the U.S. application contains a single claim directed to the shape of the bristle. In addition, for this question, assume that Frank's Japanese application was published on January 16, 2007. Which of the following is true?

(A) The Japanese patent application bars Frank's U.S. application under 102(b).

(B) Although the Japanese application discloses the same invention, there is no bar under 102(b).

    (C)   Frank will not be barred a patent based on his Japanese patent application, but he must contend with prior art by others that came into existence after March 12, 2006 because the Japanese application is for a different invention.

    (D)   Frank will not be barred a patent based on his Japanese patent application, and can claim March 12, 2006 as the effective filing date with respect to prior art by others.

149.   For this question, assume that Frank had also filed an application in Italy on September 12, 2006 that is identical in disclosure to the March 12, 2006 Japanese application. The sole claim in each relates to the novel fibers. Frank then files a U.S. application on April 1, 2007 that is identical to the two prior applications. Which of the following is true?

    (A)   Frank can claim March 12, 2006 as an earlier filing date

    (B)   Frank can claim September 12, 2006 as an earlier filing date.

    (C)   Frank cannot claim the benefit of any earlier filing date.

    (D)   Frank can claim either March 12 or September 12, 2006 as the earlier filing date, so long as he makes a specific reference to the foreign application he is claiming priority from in his U.S. application.

150. In what situations is inventorship relevant?

   (A) Determining who should win an interference proceeding.

   (B) Assessing whether a patent is barred under 102(f).

   (C) Defending against a patent infringement claim based upon a license from a co-inventor.

   (D) All of the above.

151. Which of the following best describes a joint inventor?

   (A) Someone who contributed to each of the patent claims.

   (B) Someone who contributed to at least half of the patent claims.

   (C) Someone who worked with another inventor in conceiving and reducing to practice at least one claim.

   (D) Someone who contributed to the invention of at least one claim.

152. What legal rights does a co-inventor have in a patented invention, assuming that the co-inventors are co-owners of a patent?

   (A) The right to exclude others only from any claim that the joint inventor contributed to.

   (B) The right to grant licenses, only with the consent of all joint inventors.

   (C) The right to grant licenses to the patented invention without need for approval from other joint inventors, subject to an accounting to other joint inventors.

   (D) The right to grant a license to the patented invention without need for approval or accounting to any other joint inventor.

153. What is the effect of a patent that incompletely lists the inventors, i.e., one in which an inventor is omitted, or one in which someone who does not qualify as an inventor is listed?

   (A) The patent is invalid, since an application must be filed by all inventors.

   (B) The patent may be valid if the error can be corrected through a re-examination proceeding.

   (C) Although inventorship may be corrected, only the PTO can do so during the pendency of an application.

(D) The patent may be valid if the error occurred without deceptive intent and appropriate procedures to correct the error are followed.

154. When may correction of inventorship occur, assuming other requirements for correction exist?

(A) Any time before a patent issues, but not after issuance.

(B) Any time within two years of grant of the patent.

(C) Only after a patent issues, but without limitation in time.

(D) At any time during the pendency of the application, as well as after the patent issues.

[A] Patent Rights — Scope of Rights

155. Which of the following best describes what rights a patent owner has:

   (A) The exclusive right to make and use an invention within the United States.

   (B) The exclusive right to make and use an invention within the United States and the right to exclude all others from importing the invention into the United States.

   (C) The right to exclude all others from making and using the invention within the United States.

   (D) The right to exclude all others from making, using, selling, or offering for sale the invention within the United States.

156. Bob has a patent on a new radar detector machine. Which of the following best describes what rights Bob has?

   (A) The exclusive right to make and use his machine.

   (B) The exclusive right to use his machine only.

   (C) Bob may use his patented machine without regard to state laws that govern use of radar detectors because federal patent rights govern via preemption.

   (D) Bob may exclude others from making and using his machine, but he may not be able to make and use his own machine if his machine infringes on the patent of another.

[B] Infringement — Analytical Steps

157. What (two) steps must a court take in assessing a claim for patent infringement?
ANSWER:

158. Which of the following best describes how a court should assess a claim for patent infringement against an accused product?

   (A) Compare the accused product to the patentee's product that embodies the claimed invention.

   (B) Compare the accused product to the patent claim(s).

    (C)   Construe the patent claim(s) and then compare the construed claims to the accused product.

    (D)   Compare the patent claim(s) to the claims of any patent that corresponds to the accused product.

[C]   Claim Construction

159.   Is it possible for a word to be interpreted differently in the context of interpreting the claims of different patents? Why or why not?

ANSWER:

160.   When, if ever, may extrinsic evidence be used to interpret claims?

ANSWER:

161.   Why would a dictionary or an expert witness be more relevant to interpreting claims than the testimony of the inventor?

ANSWER:

162.   Which of the following best describes the appropriate order of analysis for claim construction?

    (A)   Always evaluate the claim, specification, and file history.

    (B)   Always begin with the language of the actual claim; the specification should only be consulted if the claim language is unclear — even after considering principles of claim differentiation.

    (C)   Always begin with a dictionary definition of key terms in the claim language, followed by the claim itself, then the specification.

    (D)   Always begin with expert testimony concerning the meaning of a claim to a person of ordinary skill in the art, followed by a consideration of the specification.

163.   How does "claim differentiation" assist in claim construction?

ANSWER:

164. Which of the following is an accurate statement of how to construe claims?

   (A) Claim terms are interpreted from the perspective of an ordinary person.

   (B) Claim terms are assigned their ordinary and customary meaning to a person of skill in the art, unless the patentee has provided a different definition in the specification.

   (C) Claim terms are understood to be limited to the examples provided in the specification.

   (D) Claim terms should be interpreted without recourse to the specification, although if a claim term is unclear, resort to dictionary definitions is appropriate.

165. Which of the following is true regarding claim construction?

   (A) Claim construction is an issue of law that a court determines before discovery.

   (B) Claim construction is an issue of law that the Federal Circuit may decide *de novo* on appeal, without any deference to the decision of the district court.

   (C) Claim construction is a question of fact that the jury must decide in accordance with the Constitutional right to a jury trial.

   (D) Claim construction is a mixed question of law and fact, but may nonetheless be subject to summary judgment in some cases.

[D] Patent Infringement — General

166. X has a U.S. patent on a widget that contains components A, B, and C. X's patent claim reads: I claim a widget *comprising* A, B, and C. Which of the following is true?

   (A) X has a claim for literal infringement only against a manufacturer that makes widgets having components A, B, and C.

   (B) X has a claim for infringement against any manufacturer that makes widgets that contain A, B, and C, regardless of whether the widget contains additional elements.

   (C) X has a claim for literal infringement against any manufacturer that makes widgets are substantially identical to X's commercial product.

   (D) X has a claim for literal infringement against a manufacturer of widgets comprised solely of elements A and B if the resulting widget has the same function as X's claimed widget.

167. For the same widget invention, assume instead that the claim reads: I claim a widget *consisting* of A, B and C. Which of the following is now true?

   (A) X has a claim for literal infringement against a manufacturer that makes widgets having components A, B and C.

   (B) X has a claim for infringement against any manufacturer that makes widgets that contain A, B and C, regardless of whether the widget contains additional elements.

(C)   X has a claim for infringement against a manufacturer that makes widgets that consist solely of A and B, so long as those widgets perform the same function as X's widgets.

(D)   X has a claim for infringement against any manufacturer that makes a widget that overall has the same look and function as X's widget, regardless of whether A, B or C are included.

[E]   Doctrine of Equivalents

168.   What is the underlying policy reason for enabling a plaintiff to establish infringement at least partially using the doctrine of equivalents?

ANSWER:

169.   Which of the following is true concerning the doctrine of equivalents?

(A)   Equivalency is evaluated with regard to the entire claimed invention.

(B)   Appropriate equivalents are not limited to things known at the time of the patent application.

(C)   A claim narrowed to respond to a 112 rejection will not bar use of doctrine of equivalents because the rejection is not based on prior art.

(D)   Any amendments to patent claims raise an absolute bar to use of doctrine of equivalents.

170.   Sally has a patent with a single claim to a composition comprised of A and B. Sally sues Joe for patent infringement based upon his sale of a composition comprised of A and T. Which of the following is true?

(A)   Joe cannot infringe because he lacks element B.

(B)   Joe does not literally infringe, but he may infringe under the doctrine of equivalents if his composition is insubstantially different than Sally's to a person of skill in the art.

(C)   Joe does not literally infringe, but may infringe under the doctrine of equivalents if T is an insubstantial difference from B.

(D)   Joe does not literally infringe and cannot infringe under the doctrine of equivalents if Sally made any amendments to her claim that narrowed the scope.

171.   What is the general policy behind estopping a patentee from utilizing the doctrine of equivalents?

ANSWER:

172. Why would a patentee be estopped from using the doctrine of equivalents to establish equivalence of an element of the claimed invention?

ANSWER:

173. Which of the following describes a situation when a patentee may rebut a presumption of the surrender of subject matter?

   (A)   The patentee had no intent to surrender equivalents, as shown by testimony during litigation.

   (B)   The reason for the narrowing amendment is only tangentially relevant to the equivalent based upon the testimony of the patentee during litigation.

   (C)   The alleged equivalent would have been unforeseeable to one of skill in the art at the time of the amendment, as established through extrinsic evidence, such as expert testimony.

   (D)   The patentee could not reasonably have described the equivalent at the time the claim was narrowed because of inadequacies in the language, as shown solely by the prosecution history.

[F]   Infringement — Examples

174. Omni has a patent with a claim to 80% A, 15% B, and 5% C. Omni's competitor, Nogo makes a product that contains 81% A, 16% B, and 5% C. Can Nogo possibly infringe? Explain how.

ANSWER:

175. A has a patent on a light-emitting flying disc. B is doing research for a toy company that wants to make glowing yo-yos. B reads A's patent and carefully creates a yo-yo that emits light. B admits that but for reading A's patent, B probably would not have been able to make the yo-yo. B's yo-yo does not fall within the literal scope of A's patent claims.

   Which of the following is true?

   (A)   B is liable for infringement under the doctrine of equivalents.

   (B)   B is liable for secondary infringement.

   (C)   B is liable for derivation.

   (D)   B is not liable for infringement.

176. A has a patent on a light-emitting flying disc. B, a competitor, buys one of A's discs, studies the disc in detail and then makes its own disc. B's light-emitting flying disc does not fall within the literal claims of A's patent, specifically the claims that specify the method how light is emitted. In particular, B makes sure that his disc emits light in a novel way. However, to an undiscerning consumer, B's discs are similar to A. Does B infringe A's patent?

    (A) Yes, B infringes because he had the requisite intent to infringe.

    (B) Yes, B infringes under the doctrine of equivalents because the discs appear equivalent to a consumer and both discs emit light, although they do so in different ways.

    (C) No, B does not infringe.

    (D) Maybe, but only if B is not entitled to his own patent.

177. What is the difference between 271(b) inducement and 271(c) contributory infringement?

ANSWER:

178. When, if ever, is intent relevant to patent infringement?

ANSWER:

179. Which of the following best describes when someone will be liable for inducing infringement?

(A)   Intent to induce actions that result in direct infringement of another, regardless of whether there is any actual knowledge of the patent.

(B)   Knowledge of a patent and intent to induce infringement, regardless of whether anyone directly infringes.

(C)   Knowledge of a patent, together with action taken while a patent application is pending that induced infringement once the patent issues.

(D)   Knowledge of a patent, together with actions taken with the intent and result of inducing direct infringement by another.

180. Which of the following does *not* describe a situation where contributory infringement exists, assuming that direct infringement does exit?

(A)   Someone makes a component of a patented invention that is a material part of the invention, knowing that the component is especially made for use in infringement and not capable of substantial noninfringing use.

(B)   Someone sells a component of a patented product that constitutes a material part of the patented invention, knowing that the component is especially adapted for use in infringement and not capable of substantial noninfringing use.

(C)   Someone imports a material that is used in a patented process that is especially made for infringement and not suitable for substantial noninfringing use.

(D)   Someone offers to sell, but does not actually consummate the sale of a component of a patented invention that is a material part of the invention, knowing that the component is especially made for use in infringement and not capable of substantial noninfringing use.

181.   How is the limitation of contributory infringement to "nonstaple" components that have no insubstantial non-infringing use relevant to whether a party intends to contribute to direct infringement by another?

ANSWER:

182.   Which of the following would best describe a situation where a component was a staple article of commerce?

(A)   The patent claim is to a metal alloy containing iron and boron. The alleged contributory infringer sold iron.

(B)   The patent claim is to a uniquely shaped chair with a slipcover. The alleged contributory infringer sold the slipcover, which does not fit on any other chair.

(C)   The patent claim is to a method of reducing scars using compound excelon. The alleged contributory infringer sold compound excelon, which is an unusual chemical that is not used for any other commercial purposes.

(D)   All of the above.

FACTS FOR QUESTIONS 183-84:

Bob has a patent on a shopping cart. His arch-enemy Stan makes and sells all the components of the shopping cart in an unassembled form.

183.   Does Stan infringe Bob's patent?

(A)   No, Stan does not infringe because he does not make or sell the claimed invention.

(B)   Maybe. Stan does not literally infringe, but may infringe under the doctrine of equivalents.

(C)   Maybe. Stan does not literally infringe, but may be liable for contributory infringement or inducement of infringement, if his customers assemble the shopping cart according to Bob's claims.

(D)   Yes. Stan is liable for either contributory infringement or inducement of infringement, regardless of whether anyone else assembles the components he sells.

184.   Which of the following best describes whether Stan might be liable for inducement or contributory infringement?

(A)   Stan would be liable for contributory infringement if the individual components he sells have no substantial noninfringing use.

(B) Stan would be liable for inducement if he intended to sell the parts but had no knowledge of the patent.

(C) Stan would be liable for inducement if he knew of the patent and the individual components have no substantial noninfringing use.

(D) Stan cannot be liable for contributory infringement because he sold all the components to the patented invention, rather than a single component, regardless of whether the components he sold are staple articles.

FACTS FOR QUESTIONS 185-86:

TransBank has a patent with a claim to a method of depositing checks over the Internet with use of a scanner. Lisa has a website where she offers to sell an apparatus for scanning checks that can be used in conjunction with the Transbank patent.

185. Which of the following is true?

(A) Lisa cannot be liable to Transbank for offering to sell something that is not the entire claimed invention.

(B) Lisa may be liable for contributory infringement, but only if the apparatus is a material part of the patented method and she completes an actual sale of the apparatus.

(C) Lisa will not be liable for contributory infringement if the apparatus she sells is useful for scanning documents generally and not only for the patented method.

(D) Lisa will be liable for contributory infringement, regardless of whether anyone uses her apparatus according to the patent so long as the apparatus she offered for sale has no substantial noninfringing use.

186. Which of the following best describes whether Lisa could be liable for inducement of infringement?

(A) Lisa is liable for inducement if she intends to induce customers to buy the apparatus and use it according to the patent, regardless of whether she knows of the patent, or whether customers infringe.

(B) Lisa is liable for inducement if she knows of the patent and intends to induce infringement, regardless of whether her customers actually use the device in a manner that directly infringes.

(C) Lisa is liable for inducement if she knows of the patent, and she sells a material part to the invention.

(D) Lisa is liable for inducement if she knows of the patent, intends to induce infringement, and the customers actually do use the scanner in a way that literally infringes.

187. Paul buys a GM convertible. The convertible contains a patented top that easily opens and closes; the patent is owned by Emo, who has given GM a license to make the patented tops. Paul does not know about the patent at the time he buys the car. Which of the following is true?

   (A) Paul is liable for patent infringement if he resells the car.

   (B) Paul is not liable for patent infringement based on his purchase, but may be liable for infringement if he attempts to create a separate convertible top that is identical to the one on his convertible.

   (C) Paul is liable for patent infringement because the car he bought contains a patented part; his lack of knowledge is not a defense to direct infringement.

   (D) Paul may be liable for patent infringement, but the GM dealer will also be contributorily liable.

188. Assume that there is a patent claim for an assembled segway vehicle. If someone makes all the components of a patented segway, but sells the unassembled components to customers outside the United States, what type of liability may exist?

   (A) Direct infringement because the invention is substantially made in the United States.

   (B) Indirect infringement if there is intent to avoid infringement.

   (C) Infringement under 271(f).

   (D) Infringement under 271(g).

189. How is 271(f)(2) similar to, yet different from, 271(c)?

ANSWER:

190. Which of the following accurately states liability under 271(g)?

   (A) Someone who imports a patented process into the U.S. is liable.

   (B) Someone who imports the product of a patented process into the U.S. is liable.

   (C) Someone who imports the product of a patented process is liable only if the process is one involving biotechnology.

   (D) Someone who imports the product of a patented process into the U.S. is liable, regardless of the technology involved unless the product has been materially changed or becomes a nonessential component of another product.

191. Which of the following best describes the term of a U.S. patent that issues today?

(A)   Twenty years from the date a patent issues.

(B)   Twenty years from the date the patent application was filed.

(C)   Twenty years from the earliest effective filing date of the application.

(D)   Seventeen years from the date of the patent application.

192. On January 2, 2003, Audrey files a provisional patent application. Then, on December 11, 2003, Audrey files a nonprovisional patent application, claiming the filing date of the provisional application. Eventually, the nonprovisional application is allowed and a patent is granted on August 3, 2007. When does Audrey's patent expire?

(A)   January 2, 2023

(B)   December 11, 2023

(C)   August 3, 2024

(D)   August 3, 2027

193. On January 2, 2004, Ben files a patent application. Ben later files a continuation-in-part (CIP) application on July 27, 2004, once he obtains additional clinical data. Ben includes an explicit reference to the January 2, 2004 application before abandoning that application. Ben's CIP application is later issued as a patent on November 9, 2006. When does Ben's patent expire?

(A)   January 2, 2024.

(B)   July 27, 2024.

(C)   January 2, 2017 for claims relating to the original application and July 27, 2024 for claims based on the new clinical data.

(D)   November 9, 2026.

194. A files a patent application on February 1, 1997. The patent issues on February 1, 2001. Which of the following situations accurately describes when X would infringe A's patent?

(A)   X is liable for infringement under 271(a) for making the claimed invention from 1998-1999.

(B)   X is liable for infringement under 271(a) if X makes the claimed invention in January, 2017.

    (C)   X is liable for infringement under 271(a) if X makes the claimed invention in March, 2018.

    (D)   X is liable for infringement for infringement under 271(a) if X makes the claimed invention in 2020.

195.   When may the patent term be extended?

ANSWER:

196.   A patent is issued with a word missing in the abstract that was in the originally submitted application. Would a certificate of correction be applicable?

ANSWER:

197.   Which of the following may be changed with a properly filed certificate of correction?

   (A)   Correction of a recently discovered typographical error in the original patent specification.

   (B)   Adding a new figure to the drawings to illustrate the best mode of the invention where the best mode was not previously described.

   (C)   Adding new claims that are narrower in scope.

   (D)   Adding new test data to the specification to further support the utility of the invention.

198.   A patent is issued with a typo in the claims that was not in the originally submitted application. The typo modifies an important term that changes the scope of the claims such that they are overly broad — they would read on prior art. The typo occurred through no fault of the patent applicant. Would a certificate of correction be applicable to fix the error?

ANSWER:

199.   After Abby's patent is issued, she realizes that she forgot to include a drawing that she had created contemporaneous with the original patent application. She thinks that the issued patent probably satisfies 112, but would be more confident if the drawing was included. Assuming that the omission of the drawing was done without deceptive intent, can Abby properly obtain a reissued patent?

ANSWER:

200.   After Brenda's patent issues and she takes a patent class, she realizes that although her patent agent helped her obtain a valid patent, it fails to provide ideal coverage. In looking

over her claims, she realizes that her specification would have enabled broader claims without reading on the prior art. Assuming Brenda timely makes a motion with the requisite fee, can she reissue her patent with claims that she now feels are appropriate?

ANSWER:

201. After Cassie's snow blower patent is issued, his competitor, Donald, starts manufacturing a competing line of snow blowers. In examining his patent, Cassie realizes that his specification could have supported more specific claims that would have directly read on Donald's snow blowers. Cassie did not know that Donald was about to launch snow blowers so similar to his own invention. May Cassie properly seek a reissue application with new claims that would specifically make Donald's actions infringing?

ANSWER:

202. Which of the following describes when a reissue application may be timely sought?

(A) Within two years of issuance of the original patent for any reason.

(B) Within one year of issuance of the original patent if the patentee seeks to enlarge the scope of the claims.

(C) At any time during the patent term if the patentee seeks to enlarge the claims.

(D) At any time during the patent term if the patentee solely seeks to narrow the claims.

203. Which of the following is true in assessing whether the application is a "broadening reissue"?

(A) An application that only seeks to broaden one claim out of 50 total claims is not a broadening reissue.

(B) An application that seeks to modify a claim to broaden in one respect, but to narrow in another respect would not be considered a broadening reissue.

(C) An application that seeks to broaden a claim in any respect, even if part of the same claim is also narrowed, would raise the two-year bar.

(D) A broadening reissue is one for which the applicant seeks to broaden a substantial majority of the claims.

204. Which of the following is most accurate concerning the relevant patent term after the PTO examines a reissue application?

(A) If the application is rejected, the original patent continues in force for a term of 20 years from the date of the original patent application.

      (B)   If the application is rejected but the original patent continues in force for a period of 20 years from the date of the reissue application.

      (C)   If the patent is reissued — in original or amended form — the term is 20 years from the date of application for reissuance.

      (D)   If the patent is reissued — in original or amended form — the term is 20 years from the date of the original application.

205.   Is it possible to infringe a reissued patent during the time that the reissue application was pending?

ANSWER:

206.   Elena obtains a reissued patent with broadened claims. During the time that Elena's reissue application on a rotating ice-cream-cone holder was pending, Fred began manufacturing and selling a device similar to what was disclosed in Elena's patent. The original patent claims do not read on Fred's device, but some of the new claims do. Which of the following most accurately describes Fred's rights and/or liabilities with respect to Elena's reissued patent?

      (A)   Fred can sell the devices that he has already made without liability.

      (B)   Fred can use, but not sell the devices that he has already made.

      (C)   Fred can continue to make, use, or sell existing or new devices since he did not infringe when he first started making the devices.

      (D)   Fred can use or sell the existing devices without liability; however, whether Fred can make new devices must be determined by a court.

207.   How is the "recapture rule" for reissue applications similar to prosecution history estoppel?

ANSWER:

208.   Who can seek re-examination of a patent and when?

ANSWER:

209.   How is the current rule on what is a considered a "substantial new question of patentability" different than what was decided in *In re Portola Packaging*?

ANSWER:

210. Which of the following is a basis for permitting re-examination of a patent?

(A) A substantial new question of patentability exists based on a prior art printed publication that was previously considered by the PTO.

(B) A substantial new question of patentability exists based on allegations that the invention was offered for sale more than one year prior to the date of application.

(C) A substantial new question of patentability exists based on allegations that the best mode was not adequately disclosed.

(D) A substantial new question of patentability is raised based upon allegations of misjoinder of inventors.

211. Which of the following is true?

(A) Claims may be broadened in either a reissue or reexamination proceeding.

(B) The PTO may prompt a reexamination, but not a reissue proceeding.

(C) Only the patent owner may request a re-examination.

(D) Reissue applications may not consider issues other than anticipation and obviousness based exclusively on the content of patents and printed publications.

212. What must the plaintiff prove in a patent infringement suit?

(A) That the patent is valid and the defendant is infringing.

(B) That the patent is valid, the defendant infringes, and that the defendant is not entitled to any defenses.

(C) That the defendant infringes.

(D) That the defendant infringes and that the defendant is not entitled to any defenses.

213. Which of the following is the most accurate statement?

(A) A patent is presumed valid, but may be proved invalid, if shown by proof beyond a reasonable doubt.

(B) A patent is presumed valid, but may be proved invalid, if shown by clear and convincing evidence.

(C) A patentee has no presumption of validity; the plaintiff must prove that the patent is valid and infringed by clear and convincing evidence.

(D) A patent has no presumption of validity; rather, the patentee must first prove that the patent is valid by a preponderance of the evidence; only if the patentee is able to so does the burden then shift to the alleged infringer to show lack of infringement.

214. Which of the following is true about patent infringement litigation?

(A) If a court finds one claim invalid, all patent claims are invalid.

(B) A dependent claim is invalid if it depends upon an invalid claim.

(C) A defendant may successfully challenge a patent infringement claim by proving that the patent is invalid because the invention was in public use more than one year before the date of the application.

(D) The owner of a patent whose claims are held invalid against one party is not precluded from alleging infringement of the same claims against a different party due to the doctrine of mutuality.

215. Which of the following would be an appropriate and complete defense to patent infringement?

(A) Invalidity of the patent for failure to disclose the best mode.

(B) Invalidity of the patent for failing to claim patentable subject matter.

    (C)   Repair of the patented invention.

    (D)   Unenforceability of the patent due to inequitable conduct

    (E)   All of the above.

216.   Which of the following is a complete defense to literal infringement?

    (A)   Independent invention with no knowledge of the patent in suit.

    (B)   Common law experimental use due to use in an academic institution.

    (C)   Common law experimental use because defendant made the claimed invention purely for idle curiosity.

    (D)   Common law experimental use may be asserted by a corporation that made a claimed invention without any intent to market the composition.

217.   Bob makes a patented electric screwdriver for ten years before the patent owner, Tom, is aware of the infringement. Which of the following best describes Bob's liability?

    (A)   Tom cannot sue Bob for infringement because the statute of limitations for asserting a patent infringement claim expires six years from the date of the first infringing activity.

    (B)   Tom can sue Bob for infringement as long as he does so six years from actual knowledge of Bob's infringing activity.

    (C)   Tom can sue Bob for infringement, but he can only recover damages for the past six years.

    (D)   Tom can sue Bob for infringement, but because it has been more than six years since the infringement ensued, he is barred from monetary damages; he may, however, possibly obtain an injunction.

218.   Which of the following is most accurate?

    (A)   The doctrine of laches bars the patent owner from asserting a claim for patent infringement due to the patent owner's unreasonable delay in filing suit.

    (B)   The doctrine of laches bars the patent owner from recovery of any damages that accrued prior to the litigation, but does not entirely preclude a suit for infringement.

    (C)   The doctrine of equitable estoppel bars the patent owner from recovery of any damages that accrued prior to the litigation based upon plaintiff's misleading actions which led the defendant to believe it would not be sued.

    (D)   Both the doctrine of laches and equitable estoppel are a complete defense to a claim for infringement and prevent the patent owner from recovering any damages.

219. What is the difference between repair versus reconstruction and why does this matter in assessing liability for patent infringement?

ANSWER:

220. Gregco has a patent on a genetically modified mouse that is obese (by mouse standards). Hannah, a researcher at a major medical school, buys a mouse and genetically modifies it according to the claims in Gregco's patent. Hannah creates the mouse because there is a back-order of similar mice and she needs to meet a deadline for researching an obesity drug. Hannah's mouse falls within the claims of Gregco's patent. Will the defense of experimental use relieve Hannah of liability?

ANSWER:

221. What is the difference between asserting invalidity versus unenforceability of a patent?

ANSWER:

222. Which of the following is most accurate?

(A) Inequitable conduct that renders a patent unenforceable can only be based upon failure to disclose material prior art.

(B) Inequitable conduct is a defense that may be alleged during a re-examination proceeding, as well as in a case for patent infringement.

(C) Inequitable conduct may exist where there are misleading statements made during prosecution that are relevant to patentability.

(D) Inequitable conduct may exist based upon failure to disclose material information, even if the patent owner had no intent to deceive.

223. What remedies are a prevailing patent owner entitled to in a patent infringement suit?

ANSWER:

224. What type of monetary damages may a prevailing patent owner always obtain?

   (A) Statutory damages.

   (B) Reasonable royalty only.

   (C) Reasonable royalty or lost profits, whichever is greater.

   (D) Reasonable royalty or lost profits, whichever is less.

225. Amma is sued for patent infringement by Troll. The complaint states that Amma is making and selling a patented artificial hip joint. Troll provides health care products and plans to sell its own patented artificial hip joint. However, it does not yet have its device on the market. Amma admits making products within the scope of Troll's patent claims, but believes that the relevant claims are invalid based upon prior art not cited in the patent.

   What should Amma argue to avoid a preliminary injunction before trial?

ANSWER:

226. Which of the following is true concerning preliminary injunctions?

   (A) A likelihood of success on the merits can be presumed in a patent infringement case because patents are presumed valid in civil suits.

   (B) A patent owner is presumed to suffer irreparable harm without an injunction because the nature of a patent right is to exclude all others.

   (C) A court may grant a preliminary injunction if the balance of hardships tip in the patent owner's favor, even if the accused infringer has substantial proof that an injunction would result in bankruptcy.

   (D) The public interest factor for a patent infringement case will always favor the patent owner because the public has an interest in ensuring that valid patents are enforced.

227. Which of the following is true about monetary damages available to a prevailing patent owner?

(A) A non-manufacturing patent owner may be denied any monetary damages for failing to work the invention.

(B) A patentee is entitled to treble damages in all patent infringement cases.

(C) A patentee is entitled to either actual lost profits or statutory damages.

(D) A patentee is entitled to attorney fees if the case is considered "exceptional."

228. Which of the following may be an adequate basis for an award of attorney fees in patent litigation?

(A) A defendant's willful infringement.

(B) Litigation misconduct by either party.

(C) Inequitable conduct in obtaining the patent.

(D) All of the above.

229. How does a court determine a "reasonable royalty"?

ANSWER:

230. Why is a prevailing patent owner not entitled to claim all of the defendant's profits as "lost profits" damages?

ANSWER:

231. Which of the following would *not* be relevant to a court's decision to enhance damages under section 284?

(A) The financial condition of the defendant.

(B) Closeness of the case.

(C) Good faith belief that the patent was invalid or not infringed.

(D) Whether the defendant has been found to infringe other patents.

232. Which of the following is true concerning willful infringement?

(A) A court must provide treble damages if willful infringement is established.

(B) A court may find willful infringement, yet decline to enhance damages.

(C) A court will infer that the defendant willfully infringed if the defendant does not provide an exculpatory opinion of counsel at trial.

(D) A court may infer that the defendant willfully infringed if the defendant failed to seek advice of counsel upon notice of patent infringement.

233. Which of the following is true about the relation between marking patented inventions and damages?

   (A) If the patentee fails to mark his patented product, he cannot collect any damages.

   (B) A patentee need not mark a patented process.

   (C) A patentee need not mark his products if the patentee allows the PTO to publish its patent application, since the public would have notice of the invention.

   (D) A product is considered adequately marked for purposes of obtaining damages if the words "patent," "pat," or "patent pending," are marked on the patented article.

234. What remedies are available to a patent owner if the infringer is the federal government, or a government contractor?

ANSWER:

235. Craig applies for a patent on a new type of running shoe on January 10, 2005. The application is published 18 months after original filing date and issues with no changes to the claims on July 1, 2007. AeroMax has been making and selling a running shoe encompassed by claims of Craig's patent since 2004. Which of the following is true?

   (A) Craig can obtain damages from AeroMax since 2004.

   (B) Craig can obtain damages from AeroMax since January 10, 2005.

   (C) Craig can obtain monetary damages only since the patent issued.

   (D) Craig can obtain monetary damages since the patent issued and may also obtain a reasonable royalty for the time the patent application was pending if AeroMax had actual notice of the patent application.

PRACTICE FINAL EXAM: QUESTIONS

236. Which of the following describes patentable subject matter?

(A) A naturally occurring plant is not patentable, but a genetically modified plant is patentable subject matter.

(B) Genes — whether in their natural or isolated state — may not be patentable.

(C) A method of performing surgery is not patentable because it violates public health policy.

(D) A new game may not be patentable subject matter because it lacks utility as an invention.

237. A shaman from South Africa tells a traveler about a medicine to heal wounds that is known only within his tribe. The shaman describes the medicine in enough detail to enable the traveler, a scientist, to make the medicine on his own. The traveler does not share the shaman's information with anyone. Rather, within six months of his trip, he files a U.S. patent application, claiming the product shown to him by the shaman. There is no published prior art or patent regarding this composition. Which of the following best describes the provision of 102 under which this should be rejected?

(A) 102(a)

(B) 102(b)

(C) 102(f)

(D) All of the above.

238. Which of the following is true about patent infringement?

(A) For direct infringement to exist, all elements of a claim must be literally infringed

(B) A patent owner may not claim infringement of his invention if he does not make his own version of the claimed invention.

(C) A patent owner may not properly assert a contributory infringement claim unless the patent owner also alleges a claim against the direct infringer in the same suit.

(D) A defendant may be liable for patent infringement if a single claim is infringed, regardless of the number of other claims that are not infringed.

239. If the PTO rejects an application on the grounds of lack of enablement, what can the applicant do to overcome the objection?

    (A)   Submit information to the PTO in the form of an affidavit that would enable someone of skill in the art to practice the invention.

    (B)   Amend the application to add new information that would adequately enable someone of skill in the art to practice the invention.

    (C)   File a continuation in part application that includes additional information that would enable someone of skill in the art to practice the invention.

    (D)   Refer to an article published after her application that would explain how to use her invention.

FACTS FOR QUESTIONS 240-43:

Lisa files a U.S. application on a new widget on October 1, 2007. She conceived her invention on January 1, 2007 and reduced it to practice on March 3, 2007, in her home office in Portland, Maine.

240. Unbeknownst to Lisa, Javier reduced the same invention to practice in Peru, a WTO country, on February 1, 2006. In fact, Javier has been selling the widgets in Peru since March, 2006. Which of the following is most accurate?

    (A)   Lisa will be barred a patent under 102(a) because she was not the first person to invent the widget.

    (B)   Lisa will be entitled to obtain a patent because she is the first to file an application for the invention.

    (C)   If Javier files an application, both Lisa and Javier will be entitled to make and use the widget in the United States because they independently conceived the same invention.

    (D)   Lisa may obtain a patent regardless of Javier's prior invention, assuming that she satisfies 112 and her invention is nonobvious.

241. If Javier published a paper disclosing and enabling someone of skill in the art to make the invention on April 1, 2007, would that bar Lisa from obtaining a patent? Why or why not?

ANSWER:

242. Assume that Javier applies for a patent with claims that overlap some of the claims in Lisa's now issued patent. Which of the following is true?

(A) Lisa may oppose Javier's application.

(B) Javier can claim October 1, 2007 as its effective filing date for prior art purposes because that is the date that Lisa filed an application that disclosed the identical invention.

(C) Javier may provoke an interference with Lisa's patent, even though her patent has already issued.

(D) Javier may provoke an interference at any time after he applies for a patent, including after he is granted a patent himself.

243. What if Javier applies for and is granted a patent in his home country of Peru before Lisa applies for a U.S. patent. Is there any way that Lisa can still obtain a patent?

(A) Lisa will be barred under 102(b) if Javier's patent is granted more than one year before Lisa's reduction to practice.

(B) Lisa will be barred under 102(b) if Javier's patent is granted more than one year before Lisa's conception of the invention.

(C) Lisa will be barred under 102(b) if Javier's patent is granted more than one year before Lisa's patent application

(D) Lisa will be barred under 102(g) so long as Javier has not abandoned, suppressed, or concealed the invention.

244. Assume that the owner of a patent on a painless needle does not actually make or sell any such needles. Which of the following best describes what impact this fact has potential recovery for the owner in a patent infringement suit?

(A) All remedies are barred.

(B) No monetary damages are permitted, but injunctive relief is possible.

(C) Injunctive relief is barred, but monetary relief is possible.

(D) The patent owner is entitled to a reasonable royalty; Injunctive relief is possible, although it may be limited

245. Medway, a multinational corporation, has a patent on a catheter. Which of the following best describes a situation where Medway's patent would be infringed by the importation?

(A) Medway's claimed catheter is imported from Ireland, where Jerry has not sought patent protection.

(B) Medway's claimed catheter is imported from Japan, where it was purchased from Medway.

(C) Medway's claimed catheter is imported from Mexico, where it was sold by an authorized dealer of Medway.

(D) All of the above situations describe infringement of Medway's patent.

246. Ace has a patent with a single claim to a class of metal alloy that has high conductivity. The specification describes two types of metal alloys with high conductivity, including the alloy that the inventor believes works best. The specification does not describe other alloys in the class since the inventor has not tested any others. However, all of the other alloys in the class do in fact have high conductivity. In addition, it turns out that there is an alloy not specifically described in the specification that works better than the one the inventor noted as the best alloy. Which of the following is true?

(A) The patent is invalid based on failure to disclose the best mode since there is in fact a better alloy than the one described in the patent.

(B) The patent is invalid for lack of enablement and also failure to disclose the best mode.

(C) The patent is invalid because the claim is not enabled, but the best mode is properly disclosed.

(D) The patent satisfies the best mode and the claim is enabled by the specification.

247. A has a patent on a light-emitting flying disc. B is doing research for a toy company that wants to make glowing yo-yos. B reads A's patent and carefully creates a yo-yo that emits light. B admits that but for reading A's patent, B probably would not have been able to make the yo-yo. B's yo-yo does not fall within the literal scope of A's patent claims. Which of the following is true?

(A) B is liable for infringement under the doctrine of equivalents.

(B) B is liable for secondary infringement.

(C) B is liable for derivation.

(D) B is not liable for infringement.

FACTS FOR QUESTIONS 248-49:

Gary has a patent on a paper towel dispenser. The claimed invention is superior to the prior art in that it is capable of dispensing only one sheet at a time, thus preventing excess material from being unnecessarily unraveled. The claimed dispenser includes a rod, a rotatable spinner, and a friction disc. In particular, the claim requires an assembled dispenser for a rolled product where all these elements are combined in an operable state. Gary discovers that Knackoff is offering for sale paper towel dispenser "kits" that contain all the elements of his invention in unassembled form, together with instructions for how to assemble the claimed invention.

248. Which of the following best describes Knackoff's liability, if any, under the patent act?

(A) Knackoff infringes under 271(a) because it has substantially made the claimed invention.

(B) Knackoff does not infringe under 271(a) if Knackoff offers the kits for sale, but no one actually purchases the kits.

(C)   Knackoff does not infringe under 271(a), but is liable under 271(f).

(D)   Knackoff does not infringe under 271(a), but may be liable for infringement under 271(b).

249.   Regardless of your answer to the previous question, which of the following best describes what activity must exist for Knackoff to be liable under 271(c)?

(A)   Knackoff must intend to induce actions that would result in direct infringement by a customer, but need not be aware of the patent.

(B)   Knackoff must intend to induce infringement, but actual sale or assembly of the kits is not necessary for liability.

(C)   Knackoff must know of the patent, the elements of the kit must be non-staple items that are not capable of substantial noninfringing use, and at least one person must actually infringe by assembling the claimed invention.

(D)   Knackoff must know of the patent, intend to induce infringement, and at least one person must actually infringe by assembling the claimed invention.

250.   Bob has a patent that describes a method of making French toast. Which of the following is true?

(A)   Any chef in the United States that makes French toast infringes Bob's patent.

(B)   A box of French toast-flavored cereal would infringe the patent under the doctrine of equivalents.

(C)   Bob cannot assert the patent against someone that has been making French toast longer than Bob has been alive, since such an individual would have learned the method independent of Bob's patent.

(D)   Bob's ability to enjoin others from making French toast depends on the scope of the claim(s) of his patent.

FACTS FOR QUESTIONS 251-52:

Mitch and Sally are two scientists that work for Acme Pharmaceuticals, but in different departments; as employees of Acme, they are required to assign all rights they have in patents and patent applications. Mitch files an application disclosing a new class of chemical compounds on April 1, 2006, which is published on September 15, 2007. Although Mitch discloses an entire class, he only claims one compound within the class.

251. Sally files a patent application claiming a different compound within Mitch's class of claimed compounds than the one Mitch claimed. Her application is filed on October 1, 2007. She has not yet reduced her invention to practice, but her application adequately discloses her compound to enable one of skill in the art to make and use her claimed compound. Mitch's application is still pending at the time that Sally's application is filed. Which of the following is true?

   (A) Sally's invention is barred under 102(a).

   (B) Sally's invention is not barred by 102(a), but is barred by 102(e).

   (C) Sally's invention is not barred under 102 by Mitch's application since it does not claim her invention, but could be barred under 103.

   (D) Sally's invention is not barred under 102 by Mitch's application and also would not be barred under 103 since both applications are assigned to Acme.

252. Walt works for Valley Pharma. He files an application on August 9, 2007 claiming a compound that is not within the class that Mitch describes, but may be obvious based upon the class Mitch describes. At the time of Walt's application, he did not know about Mitch's application. However, the compounds created by Walt and Mitch were both done as a result of activities undertaken under a joint research agreement between valley and Acme. Which of the following is true?

   (A) Mitch's application is not relevant prior art because Mitch's application was not publicly available until after Walt filed his application.

   (B) Mitch's application would be relevant prior art, but Walt's claimed invention would not be considered obvious based upon Mitch's application because of the joint research agreement.

   (C) Mitch's application would be relevant prior art and Walt's claimed invention may be considered obvious in light of Mitch's application since regardless of the joint research agreement, the applications are assigned to different companies.

   (D) Mitch's application would not be relevant prior art because Walt can claim the benefit of Mitch's priority date since they are part of team of inventors working on developing new compounds subject to a joint research agreement.

253. Which of the following is true about patent infringement litigation?

   (A) A dependent claim is invalid if the independent claim from which it depends is adjudicated as invalid.

(B)   The owner of a patent whose claims are held invalid may assert the same claims against a different party in a new lawsuit.

(C)   If a court finds that all claims of a patent was procured through inequitable conduct, it is considered unenforceable against the defendant in that case, as well as all future cases.

(D)   Independent invention, together with no actual knowledge of the patent in suit, is a complete defense to patent infringement.

FACTS FOR QUESTIONS 254-56:

Luke has a patent on a spaceship. Luke's patent describes the importance of using Kypton, a relatively new compound that is light-weight, but also excellent insulation against heat and cold. Leah wants to make a spaceship and reads a number of patents, including Luke's. She makes her own spaceship in outer space to avoid any potential claims of infringement. She does not use Kypton for her spaceship, but, rather, comes up with a new and nonobvious compound, Lipton.

254.   Leah imports one of her completed spaceships into the U.S. so that it may be tested. Which of the following is true?

(A)   Leah is not liable for patent infringement because she made her ship in outer space.

(B)   Leah may be liable for infringement, even if her ship does not use Kypton, if she literally infringes all the elements of Luke's claim except Kypton and Lipton is an insubstantial difference from Kypton.

(C)   Leah may properly defend against an infringement claim if she obtains her own patent for a spaceship using her Lipton compound.

(D)   Leah is not liable for patent infringement if she has not yet sold, or offered for sale her spaceship.

255.   Assume that Leah truly was the first person to create the Lipton compound, such that it did not exist at the time that Luke created his spaceship. Which of the following is true?

(A)   Luke cannot rely on the doctrine of equivalents for alleging that Leah infringes.

(B)   Leah cannot infringe because her claimed invention would be new.

(C)   Leah would infringe a claim that used the language "means for insulating" if Lipton is equivalent to one of the "means for insulating" that was described in Luke's patent specification.

(D)   Leah may infringe a claim to the spaceship where Kypton is specifically included as an element if Lipton is deemed an insubstantial equivalent.

256.   Leah begins to sell her spaceship. She embarks on a major advertising campaign and appears in all the ads. Her marketing director thinks that her presence might help since she is an attractive and articulate woman. Leah does as suggested since she has never before attempted to sell any products. To her great delight, she receives many purchase orders, as well as fan mail. She also receives many requests to negotiate licenses, although no licenses have yet been consummated. She also receives an office action from the PTO, rejecting her application as obvious in light of Luke's patent. Which of the following best describes her situation?

(A)   Leah may overcome the PTO rejection by disclaiming Krypton in her claims.

(B)   Leah's invention is nonobvious because the purchase orders indicate commercial success.

(C)   Leah cannot establish nonobviousness because commercial success and licensing activity do not establish a majority of the secondary consideration factors.

(D)   Leah most likely does not have any secondary considerations of nonobviousness that she can use to rebut the PTO rejection.

FACTS FOR QUESTIONS 257-58:

Jared has a patent on a coffee container that can be easily transported since it has handles at the top of the outer shell, and also can be used to pour coffee out of a spout that is connected to a flexible bag within the outer shell. The patent describes the invention as an important advance over the prior art because it has a better center of gravity than other inventions, although the claims do not mention center of gravity as an element. The claims also are not restricted to coffee; they broadly claim a container for holding liquid. Jared sues Charbucks for patent infringement, alleging that the coffee container that Charbucks sells to customers who want a dozen cups of coffee "on the go" infringes its patent.

257.   Charbucks alleges that the patent is invalid as obvious over a number of pieces of prior art. Charbucks claims that boxes of wine with a spout for dispensing wine constitute relevant prior art because they were sold prior to the claimed invention. In addition, Charbucks claims a patented golf club as analogous prior art because the patent describes the importance of having a center of gravity. Which of the following is true?

(A)   Both items identified by Charbucks are analogous prior art that may be considered for obviousness.

(B)   The items identified by Charbucks may not be considered for obviousness unless Jared had actual knowledge of them in creating his invention.

(C)   The wine box would be analogous prior art, but not the golf club patent.

(D)   The golf club patent is a type of relevant prior art (patent), but is not analogous, such that it cannot be used; the public use of the wine box does not constitute prior art because the use is by a third party.

258.   Which of the following best describes whether the alleged prior art could be permissibly considered by a court in the litigation action?

(A)   The court cannot consider either reference if it was not previously considered by the USPTO.

(B)   The court cannot consider the wine container in assessing whether the invention was obvious because the wine container does not have handles, unlike the claimed invention.

(C)   The court should find the patent as invalid if either reference alone, or together establish the claimed invention is obvious beyond a reasonable doubt.

(D)   The court can consider all evidence and find the patent obvious, even if the PTO has re-examined the patent based on the references noted by Charbucks and found the patent valid over those references.

259.   On February 15, 2006, Danielle files a provisional patent application. On December 15, 2006, Danielle files a nonprovisional patent application, claiming the filing date of the provisional application. The nonprovisional application is allowed and the patent issued on May 1, 2007. When does the patent expire?

(A)   February 15, 2026.

(B)   December 15, 2026.

(C)   May 1, 2027.

(D)   May 1, 2024.

FACTS FOR QUESTIONS 260-61:

On January 2, 2004, Barry files a patent application for a brush made completely of rubber. The disclosure discusses the inventor's motivation for designing a brush that could detangle and remove pet hair without inflicting unnecessary pain on the pet. The specification states that other uses of the brush will be known to those of skill in the art. The specification does not elaborate on other uses, besides to say that it can be safely used as a human hairbrush. The claims only describe the physical structure of the brush.

260.   Barry later discovers that although his initial prototype was made of rubber, other flexible materials will work. Accordingly, on January 2, 2006, Barry files a CIP. The CIP is identical in disclosure to the 2004 application except for additional information on how to make and use brushes with other flexible materials besides rubber. In particular, the patent claims a brush made of rubber, as well as a brush made of any flexible material. The CIP specifically makes a reference to the earlier application and claims the benefit of that priority date. Which of the following is true about examination of the CIP application?

(A)   The CIP application should be rejected because the new information constitutes impermissible new matter added to the application.

(B)   The USPTO will use January 2, 2006 as the date of invention for claims to any flexible material, but will use the earlier date for claims to rubber brushes.

(C)   The USPTO will use January 2, 2004 as the date of invention for all claims because Barry satisfied the requirement of section 120 — the earlier application was copending, he is the same inventor, and the disclosures are identical except for the additional information on flexible materials.

(D)   The USPTO will use January 2, 2006 at the date of invention for all claims because that is the date the CIP application was filed.

261.   The CIP is published on July 15, 2007 and issues as a patent on December 1, 2007. When does the patent expire?

(A)   January 2, 2024.

(B)   January 2, 2026.

(C)   January 2, 2024 for claims relating to rubber brushes and January 2, 2026 for claims relating to new brushes.

(D)   December 1, 2027.

262.   Barry later discovers that a cleaning company is using his brush to clean upholstery and rugs. Which of the following best describes whether the company is liable?

(A)   The cleaning company infringes because it is using Barry's patented invention.

(B)   The cleaning company does not infringe because it is using the brush for a different purpose than the one Barry described in his patent.

(C)   The cleaning company may avoid liability if it purchased the brush from someone Barry authorized to sell the brush.

(D)   The cleaning company may continue to use the brush without liability if Barry does not initiate litigation until six years after he is aware of their action.

263.   The cleaning company purchases brushes directly from Barry. Some of the bristles of the brushes break off. The company decides to try to fix the brushes, rather than buy new ones. Which of the following is true?

(A)   The company is not liable for infringement because it purchased the brushes directly from Barry.

(B)   The company is not liable for infringement because it is only repairing a part of the brush, and not making the entire patented invention.

(C)   The company may be liable for infringement only if Barry has claims to the bristles themselves.

(D)   The company may be liable for infringement if the brush had outlived its expected life span and the repair involves heating the brush and adding additional rubber to create new bristles.

FACTS FOR QUESTIONS 264-65:

Daffy invents a car that helps clean the air, rather than pollute it. She immediately writes about her invention on her friend's blog, describing all elements of her invention in great detail. Eighteen months after her invention, Daffy files a patent application for her invention.

264. Prior to Daffy's invention, no one had ever created or described her car. Which of the following best describes whether the invention is patentable?

    (A) Daffy's invention is anticipated pursuant to 102(a).

    (B) Daffy is not barred by 102(a), but is barred a patent by 102(b).

    (C) Daffy is not barred by 102(a) and although there is a printed publication more than one year before her application, it does not count against her because it is not authored by another.

    (D) Daffy is not barred by 102(a) or 102(b); although she wrote about her invention, the blog entry was not "published," such that there is not patent-defeating printed publication.

265. Which of the following best describes whether Daffy could establish that her invention is not barred by 102(b)?

    (A) An affidavit by someone of skill in the art states that Daffy's car was novel and nonobvious at the time of her invention.

    (B) Daffy was conducting experiments with a single car that was always within her control.

    (C) Daffy was experimenting with different embodiments to see what would be the most marketable version of her car.

    (D) Daffy cannot negate the 102(b) bar.

266. George develops a new blender July 15, 2006, but does not submit a U.S. patent application until July 2, 2007. Kitty separately develops the identical blender in Korea; she actually reduces to practice the blender on July 1, 2006. Kitty thereafter files a patent application in Korea on August 1, 2006. Kitty files a U.S. patent application on January 15, 2007, which is published on December 1, 2007. Her application describes the blender that George claims in his application, although her claims differ from George's. Which of the following best describes how an examiner would view George's application on December 2, 2007.

    (A) Kitty's prior blender will bar George under 102(a).

    (B) Kitty's prior Korean application will bar George from obtaining a patent under 102(d).

    (C) Kitty's prior U.S. application will bar George under 102(e).

    (D) Kitty's blender will bar George from obtaining a patent under 102(g)(2).

267. Which of the following statements is most accurate concerning correction of patents?

    (A) Anyone can seek a reissue or reexamination of a patent.

    (B) A re-examination must be requested within two years of the patent grant.

    (C) A reissue proceeding may result in the complete loss of a patent.

    (D) Re-examination may be properly granted based on lack of proper subject matter.

268. Martin has a widget patent with one claim that reads: I claim a widget consisting of A, B, and C. Which of the following best describes what would constitute infringing activity by Elaine?

    (A) Import widgets that consist of A, B, and C.

    (B) Make widgets containing A, B, C, and D, but only if Elaine has a patent for widgets with those four elements.

    (C) Make widgets consisting of A, B, C, and D, regardless of whether Elaine has its own patent.

    (D) All of the above would constitute infringing activity by Elaine.

269. Martin has a widget patent with one claim that reads: I claim a widget comprising A, B, and C. Which of the following describes a situation in which Elaine would infringe X's widget claim?

    (A) Elaine sells widgets that contain A and C.

    (B) Elaine sells widgets that contain A, B, and D, where Elaine's widgets overall perform the same function as X's widgets.

    (C) Elaine's widgets that contain A, B, and D, where elements C and D perform the same function, but in a different way.

    (D) Elaine sells widgets that contain A, B, C, and D.

FACTS FOR QUESTIONS 270-71:

Hank files an application for a patent in France on a new windshield wiper system on March 1, 2006. Hank's application discloses wipers that have a new shape, as well as a newly automated system that the driver need not manually initiate. The French application contains claims only directed to the automation system. Hank files a U.S. application on April 1, 2007 that has the same disclosure as the French application, but only contains claims directed at the new shape of the wipers. The U.S. application does not refer to the earlier French application.

270. Six months after the U.S. application is filed, but before any office action is issued by the USPTO, the French patent application is published. Which of the following best describes the impact of the French application on his U.S. application?

    (A) Hanks' U.S. application cannot claim the benefit of the March 1, 2006 date because he did not include a specific reference to the French application.

    (B)   Hank's U.S. application is not barred by the French application because it was not published until after he filed the U.S. application.

    (C)   Hank's U.S. application is not barred by the French application and he can claim the benefit of the March 1, 2006 priority date with respect to all prior art.

    (D)   Hank's U.S. application is not barred by the French application, but he cannot claim the benefit of the earlier priority date because the French application claims a different invention.

271.   What if prior to Hank's French application, he had first filed an application in Hungary with a similar disclosure on February 1, 2005. The Hungarian application never became a patent because it claimed unpatentable subject matter. The application nonetheless was published on September 1, 2006. Which of the following is true?

    (A)   The Hungarian patent application constitutes 102(b) prior art because it is a valid type of prior art that was publicly accessible more than one year before Hank's U.S. application.

    (B)   The Hungarian patent application does not constitute 102(b) prior art if Hank claims entitlement to the French application date.

    (C)   The Hungarian patent application does not constitute 102(b) prior art because Hank is entitled to claim February 1, 2004 as the priority date pursuant to section 119.

    (D)   The Hungarian patent application bars the U.S. application under 102(d).

272.   If Hank is ultimately issued a patent for his new windshield wiper system. Which of the following best describes the patent term?

    (A)   20 years from the date the patent issues, regardless of whether Hank is entitled to claim the benefit of an earlier filing date.

    (B)   20 years from March 1, 2006, if Hank is entitled to use this earlier filing date.

    (C)   20 years from April 1, 2007, even if Hank is entitled to an earlier filing date for prior art purposes, since there is no earlier U.S. application date.

    (D)   17 years from the date the patent issues, regardless of whether Hank is entitled to claim the benefit of an earlier filing date.

273.   Which of the following is true concerning reissue of a patent?

    (A)   A reissue application has a heightened statutory presumption of validity because it has been reviewed twice by the PTO.

    (B)   Reissue applications are only proper if the patentee seeks to narrow the claims.

    (C)   A patent that is subject to reissue examination is not enforceable unless and until it is reissued.

    (D)   A reissue proceeding is proper if an applicant makes a clerical error in the spelling of the inventors.

274. Claudia has a patent on composition X. The patent specification describes X as a biological material that is useful for treating tumors. The patent claims, however, only refer to the chemical composition of X and do not refer to its utility. After Claudia's patent issues, Donald, a research scientist, buys a sample of X from a licensed manufacturer of Claudia. Using the purchased sample, Donald discovers that X is useful as a remedy for baldness when applied directly to hairless areas. Which of the following is most accurate?

    (A) Donald does not infringe Claudia's patent.

    (B) Donald does not infringe Claudia's patent and may obtain a method patent regarding X, assuming that the method is novel and nonobvious.

    (C) Donald infringes Claudia's patent and is barred from obtaining a patent for his discovery.

    (D) Donald infringes Claudia's patent, but has a strong argument for invalidity based on lack of utility since Claudia's patent fails to disclose X's utility as a method for treating baldness.

275. Melatonin is a natural substance that has been known for decades and even available for purchase by consumers in tablet form. Theresa discovers that in addition to the typically touted merits of melatonin as a sleep aid, it improves short-term memory. Which of the following is true?

    (A) Theresa cannot obtain a patent because she has only made an observation, and not a patentable invention.

    (B) Theresa cannot obtain a patent because melatonin anticipates her invention.

    (C) Theresa cannot obtain a patent on melatonin, but can obtain a patent for a method of using melatonin.

    (D) Theresa can obtain a patent with claims to both a melatonin composition, as well as a method of using the composition because prior art does not disclose use of melatonin for memory improvement.

276. If someone were to invent a car that could truly go backwards or forwards in time, would they be barred a patent based upon the 1980s movie *Back to the Future*, in which there is a car that purportedly does these things? Why or why not?

ANSWER:

277. Company Zano has a patent with a single claim to a new chemical composition. The patent specification describes in detail how to make the composition, as well as how to use it to treat arthritis, including some preliminary clinical tests. However, later tests conducted after the application is filed show that although not toxic, the composition

was no better than a placebo in treating arthritis. On the other hand, the composition was found to promote hair growth. Which of the following is true?

(A) The patent is invalid for lack of enablement since it fails to enable one of skill in the art to effectively treat arthritis symptoms.

(B) The patent is invalid for failure to disclose the best mode since use of the claimed invention for promoting hair growth is not disclosed.

(C) The patent is invalid for lack of utility since the disclosed use is not a clinically superior treatment for arthritis.

(D) None of the above is true.

278. Jack and Jill are professors at Sunny State School of Medicine. While doing research on hepatitis, they experiment with a battery of different pre-existing chemical compounds, including Zano's patented composition, which they make in their research lab. They discover that Zano's patented composition is useful for treating hepatitis, a use that is not disclosed in Zano's patent. Which of the following is true?

(A) Jack and Jill are liable for direct infringement of Zano's patent.

(B) Jack and Jill technically infringe, but have a complete defense based upon common law experimental use.

(C) Jack and Jill technically infringe, but have a complete defense based upon statutory experimental use.

(D) Jack and Jill infringe, but will likely prevail in an infringement suit if they challenge the patent as invalid for failure to disclose utility in treating hepatitis.

FACTS FOR QUESTIONS 279-80:

The plant Ocam is a naturally occurring plant native to sub-Saharan Africa. Natives of the region have been eating the plant for years when food is scarce since it minimizes hunger pains. Judy brings back some Ocam from vacation. Ocam does not exist in the United States.

279. Which of the following best describes whether Judy can obtain a patent based upon Ocam and what type(s) of patent(s) she could obtain?

(A) Judy can obtain a patent for Ocam if she is the first person to discover the properties of Ocam in the United States.

(B) Judy cannot obtain a patent for naturally occurring Ocam, but may be able to obtain a patent on a purified version of Ocam that is more concentrated than the natural plant.

(C) Judy cannot obtain a patent on naturally occurring Ocam, or on the purified version, regardless of whether the purified version is more concentrated since Judy did not make an invention.

(D) Judy may be able to obtain a patent on a method of using natural Ocam, as well as a patent on a purified version of Ocam.

280.   Judy creates a synthetic variant of Ocam in the lab that also is effective at minimizing
        hunger pains and can be packaged easily in tablet forms for weight loss. Jill files a
        patent application for her synthetic composition. Which of the following is true,
        assuming that there is no prior art beyond what is mentioned in this question?

   (A)   Jill will be barred a patent based on 102(b) since the invention was in public use.

   (B)   Jill will be barred a patent under 102(a) because of the natural Ocam.

   (C)   Jill will not be barred under 102(a), but her invention may be obvious.

   (D)   Jill will not be barred under 102(a) and her invention is not obvious in light of
         the prior art.

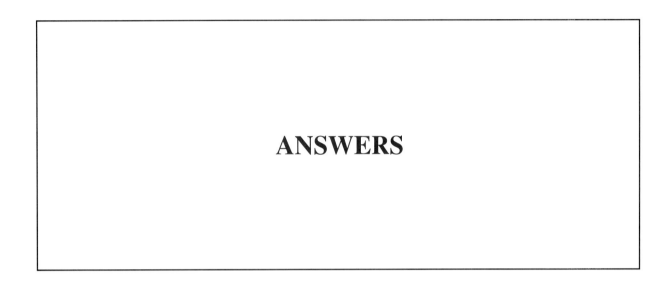

ANSWERS

1. **The best answer is A**. The categories listed in this Answer correspond to the categories listed under Section 101. While the United States Supreme Court has stated that "anything under the sun made by man" is patentable in *Diamond v. Chakrabarty*, it also said that subject matter must nonetheless fall within *a* category under the statutory section of subject matter. Accordingly, **Answer B is incorrect** as an incomplete answer. **Answer C is incorrect** because the statute explicitly states that "any new and useful process" may be patentable. There is no exclusion from patentability for new methods of using known compositions. **Answer D is incorrect** because it is inconsistent with the statutory language on patentable subject matter under Section 101. The statute provides that patents are available for "new and useful *improvement*" of any of the categories of patentable subject matter.

2. **The best answer is D**. The claim at issue before the Supreme Court was a genetically modified — and still living — bacteria. One argument that the claim should be denied was that living matter were per se unpatentable, but a 5-4 majority of the Supreme Court rejected this idea. The Supreme Court was not persuaded by suggestions that granting patents would result in a "parade of horribles," or that explicit authority from Congress was required to embrace matter that did not exist at the time the Patent Act was enacted. Methods of inoculating bacteria were considered patentable in the same case, but were not at issue before the Supreme Court. Accordingly **C is incorrect**. In addition, the Supreme Court clarified that observation of physical phenomena and biological products in their natural state were unpatentable subject matter, such that **Answers A and B are incorrect**.

3. **The best answer is A** because although the United States Supreme Court has never explicitly ruled on this, the Federal Circuit, as well as the USPTO, currently consider such methods to be patentable. *State Street Bank* together with *AT&T v. Excel* are considered the key Federal Circuit opinions that opened the judicial doors to permitting patentable subject matter. *State Street Bank* claimed that there was no prior bar to patenting such matter and that the perceived bar was based on cases where the methods were found patentable on other grounds, such as novelty and obviousness. Mere algorithms or scientific principles are never considered patentable as observations of natural phenomena. Accordingly, **Answers C and D are incorrect**. Computer software may be subject to copyright protection, but that does not preclude the existence of patent protection. Rather, computer software may be patentable under both patent and copyright laws, so **Answer B is incorrect**.

4. **The best answer is C**. A sandwich of any sort is a patentable *subject matter* in that it is a product that could constitute a composition of matter. Although such a sandwich

may not be ultimately granted a patent, that would be on grounds of novelty or nonboviousness and not on the basis of patentable subject matter. In addition, depending on what type of sandwich is *claimed*, it may be possible to obtain a patent. In particular, an inventor did receive a patent for a sandwich with a special crust and a filling that could comprise elements such as peanut butter and jelly — as well as other fillings that were more nontraditional. Even if some products seem unpatentable, it is important to be able to evaluate the proper basis — if any. Patentable subject matter is the first, but not the only, criterion that must be satisfied for patentability.

Answer A is incorrect. There is nothing in the Patent Act that suggests that subject matter that could potentially be patented under another scheme cannot be given patent protection. In fact, genetically modified plants may face challenges under some of these other provisions which were intended to address plants cultivated without biotechnology — they must be either sexually or asexually reproduced.

Answer D is also incorrect since there is no requirement that the applicant establish that the invention falls within a specific statutory category of patentable subject matter.

Answer B is incorrect, although probably the trickiest false answer. There is no per se exclusion for any method. In addition, while the prospect that a patent might bar medical treatment may sound problematic, there is currently nothing in the Patent Act to provide a basis for excluding such subject matter. In addition, although there is dicta in older cases about a morality requirement, that is for the requirement of utility and is no longer a valid grounds for rejecting otherwise useful inventions. However, if your instinct suggests that this should not be patentable, you are in agreement with many countries beyond the United States. For example, many countries in Europe have a bar on patenting medical procedures. In addition, although the United States permits patenting such procedures, most such procedures are not *enforceable* against doctors due to an amendment of the patent laws in the late 1990s as a result of a high profile case, *Pallin v. Singer*, involving a surgeon who was sued for patent infringement. The enforceability provision is in 35 U.S.C 287(c), but only the direct infringer — the doctor — is immune from liability, such that secondary liability is still theoretically possible.

5. A design patent is granted for a "new, original and ornamental *design* for an article of manufacture," under section 171 — a different provision than the patentable subject matter provision used for utility patents. The basic difference is that utility patents are for inventions that are functional (hence, the term "utility") whereas design patents provide protection for what is not functional. For example, a special shape of a bottle, or the sole of a shoe could be subject to protection under a design patent if it is solely ornamental and not functional. The term for design patents is shorter than for utility patents (14 years from grant versus 20 years from the effective filing date).

6. **The best answer is C.** A medical device may be considered useful from a patent perspective, regardless of whether it is considered useful in a commercial setting. In addition, patentable utility does not consider whether a composition satisfies criteria of other agencies, such as the FDA, such that **Answer B is incorrect**. Similarly, so long as the patentable composition is useful for its stated purpose, increased efficaciousness over prior compositions is not required, such that **Answer A is incorrect**. **Answer D is wrong because only one answer is correct**.

7. **The best answer is D** because it is the most complete answer. **Answer B is incorrect** because it only states part of the requirement of utility. **Answer C is incorrect** because morality is no longer part of the requirement of utility. Finally, **Answer A is incorrect**, because utility does not require technical subject matter.

8. **The best answer is C.** For utility patents, an invention must have some practical — as opposed to aesthetic or psychological — utility. The invention need not be commercially valuable, or even applicable to a commercial enterprise. Indeed, entertainment devices and pet-grooming devices have been deemed patentable. Based on these criteria, a toy that has utility for toddlers and utility for the caretaker of a toddler would seem to easily satisfy the requirement. On the other hand, **Answers A and B are incorrect** because they do not demonstrate any practical utility. The utility must be "substantial and credible." **Answer D is incorrect** because any product could theoretically be used as a door stop.

9. **The best answer is C.** An invention may satisfy the statutory standard of utility without being useful in all possible settings. In addition, an invention only needs one credible use. **Answer D is incorrect** because there is no present utility; similarity to a different compound that is useful is not sufficient. **Answers A and B are incorrect** because an invention cannot be useful if it fails to perform as intended. Accordingly, if an invention purports to move perpetually but cannot actually do so, it has no utility.

[A] Applications

10. **The best answer is A.** The major distinction between a provisional and nonprovisional application is that the provisional lacks claims. The provisional application may be filed to enable an applicant to claim the date of the provisional application when the nonprovisional application is filed up to one year later. There is also a lower fee for provisional applications, but that is not the primary distinction.

   Answer D is incorrect since there is a distinction beyond a lower fee, although there is admittedly a lower fee for provisional applications. **Answer B is incorrect** since there is a filing fee for even provisional applications. **Answer C is incorrect** because although drawings may be included in either type of application, they are never required for either.

11. **The best answer is D.** The provisional application serves as a place holder with respect to claiming a priority date with respect to prior art. Prior art that exists between the date of the provisional and non-provisional application will not be counted against the applicant. In this way, a provisional application is somewhat analogous to a "intent to use" trademark application that serves as a place holder with respect to subsequent applications.

   Answer A is incorrect because provisional applications do not convert into non-provisional applications. In addition, the non-provisional applications must have claims that by definition do not need to exist in the provisional application. **Answer B is also incorrect** because there is no automatic conversion to a continuation application. Rather, a continuation application is an application based upon the same specification of a previously filed non-provisional application. An applicant whose claims have been finally rejected may elect to file a continuation application in order to continue the examination process.

   Answer C is also incorrect because the PTO does not examine provisional applications. The applicant must file a nonprovisional application if the applicant wants the PTO to examine its application.

12. **The best answer is B.** An applicant of a provisional application may mark a product patent *pending*, but may not mark the product as patented. Furthermore, incorrectly marking the product consitutes false marking, which may result in liability under 35 U.S.C. 292. All other statements are true, such that **Answers A, C, and D are incorrect**.

13. **The best answer is D.** First, provisional applications are never published, so **Answers B and C are incorrect** in treating all applications alike. Answer B is also incorrect

because the relevant time period is from the earliest effective filing date. **Answer A is incorrect** because some non-provisional applications are published. Although most applications are published within 18 months from filing, there are situations where the applications are not published. For example, if the invention is subject to a secrecy order under 35 U.S.C 181, it would not be published. A more typical reason for not publishing the invention is when the applicant requested non-publication and certified that the disclosed invention is not and will not be the subject of application, which does require publication of applications 18 months from filing.

[B]   Claims

14. Claims are essential in defining the invention. A well-drafted claim is essential to ensuring that the claimed invention is patentable over prior art. In addition, claims are key for infringement since broader claims — so long as they are properly supported by the specification and valid over the prior art — can cover a wider range of infringing activity.

15. **The best answer is D**. A claim is intended to describe the elements of the invention in a manner that enables the USPTO to ascertain whether the invention is patentable over prior art. In addition, the elements of a patent claim will enable competitors to ascertain the scope of patent rights. **Answers A–C are incorrect** because they describe what an *application* must disclose, but not the claim itself. In particular, the specification must disclose the utility and patentability (including 102, 103, and 112) of the invention. However, the claim itself does not need to assert its utility or benefit over prior art.

16. Although the body of the claim, typically consisting of the structural elements of the invention, is important, the transition phrase is key to both assessing its patentability over prior art, as well as its scope for infringement. In particular, if the term "consisting" is used, the invention is limited to only the specified elements. Accordingly, infringement does not exist unless someone has only those elements; if someone has all the claimed elements *plus* an additional one, there is typically no infringement. On the other hand, the term "comprising" means that the invention contains all the stated elements, but is not limited to those elements. Accordingly, someone can infringe if they have all the claimed elements, plus additional ones. Although "comprising" is typically preferred for broader scope, it is sometimes not possible in a crowded prior art field. A third type of transition, "consisting essentially of" is also alternatively used when "comprising" is not possible. However, the scope of this phrase is unclear beyond being between the scope of "consisting" and "comprising."

17. **The best answer is D**. The preamble is typically short — it may be as short as just a few words; for example, the preamble may state "A plane," such that **Answer A is incorrect**. On the other hand, there are no mandatory limits and preambles sometimes are longer to emphasize a necessary limit to distinguish the invention over the prior art, such that **Answer B is incorrect. Answer C is also incorrect** because although the preamble probably describes an invention within statutory classifications, those

actual classifications need not be used. For example, even though a patentable invention may be a composition or manufacture, neither term needs to be used in the preamble. Finally, if the preamble contains qualifying language, it *may* potentially limit the scope of the claim.

18.   Generally, the preamble limits the claim scope if it recites essential elements, or is necessary to give meaning to the claim. If a preamble is short and the body of the claim describes a complete invention with no missing elements, the preamble is not likely to limit the scope. A recitation of an intended purpose in the claim is probably not limiting if the body recites a complete structure.

19.   **The best answer is D**. A dependent claim is one that *depends on* an independent claim. Typically, the dependent claim will specifically refer to the independent claim by number. For example, the dependent claim may read: "The widget of claim 4 wherein the widget further comprises. . . ." Since the dependent claim refers back to the independent claim, it is essentially a short-hand way of including all of the elements of the independent claim.

      Answer A is incorrect because there is no requirement that applications contain both independent and dependent claims (although most applications typically do), since all independent claims would likely become cumbersome if there were many elements.

      Answers B and C are incorrect because the validity of claims is not linked to whether they are dependent or independent. The validity of the independent claim does not mean the dependent claim is valid. A sometimes tougher issue to understand is that dependent claims can be valid even if the independent claim from which it depends is invalid. This is expressly stated in Section 282 of the Patent Act, which states that "each claim of a patent (whether in independent, dependent, or multiple dependent form) shall be presumed valid independently of the validity of other claims; dependent or multiple dependent claims shall be presumed valid even though dependent upon an invalid claim." This should seem reasonable if you consider dependent claims simply a way to incorporate all the elements without re-stating them in full. Accordingly, if the independent claim was too broad to be patentable over prior art, it is entirely possible that the narrower dependent claim would nonetheless be patentable.

20.   The general principle is that where there is a dependent claim, the independent claim from which the dependent claim derives is assumed not to include the limitations in the dependent claim.

21.   **The best answer is B**. Typically, an applicant has two opportunities to respond to office actions before the USPTO issues a "final" rejection. Since the applicant has two opportunities, **Answer A is incorrect**. In addition, the applicant may amend some, all, or none of the claims at this time. The applicant may alternatively chose to simply defend its initial claims. **Answers C and D are incorrect** because it is not necessary to choose between responding and appealing. In fact, appeal is not even appropriate unless and

until there is a final office action. Similarly, there is no need to file a continuation application unless and until there is a final office action and the applicant wants to continue the examination process.

[A]   General

22.   **The best answer is B**. Although the requirements of 112 relate to the invention, they are all fundamentally tied to the *application* — as opposed to the invention. Accordingly, the time of application is appropriate. **Answers A, C, and D are incorrect** because all other times are not relevant to 112. However, the time of invention may be relevant to other questions of validity, such as 102 anticipation.

23.   **No**. The requirements of 112 must be satisfied as of the filing date of the application. In addition, new information added to an application — other than a continuation-in-part application — constitutes impermissible new matter under 132.

24.   **The best answer is D. Answer B is incorrect** because it is not as comprehensive. **Answer C is incorrect** because it is overbroad — foreign patents, although publicly available, may not be used to satisfy 112 disclosure requirements. Although foreign patents may be used to satisfy some aspects of 112, those do not include paragraphs one, two, or six of Section 112.

[B]   Section 112 Disclosure — Enablement

25.   **The best answer is B**. A specification must enable others of skill in the art to both make and use the invention, such that **Answer A is incorrect. Answer D is incorrect** because the relevant person is one of "skill in the art," and not any person. There is no per se rule about what must be included in the actual specification. Although working examples are typical, they are not mandatory, such that **Answer C is incorrect**.

26.   **No**. The requirements are independent. An application satisfies the written description requirement so long as the applicant adequately demonstrates that the applicant was in possession of the claimed invention as of the filing date of the application. However, even if this is accomplished, the application may not provide adequate direction to those of skill in the art to both make and use the invention and if it fails to do so, enablement will not be satisfied.

27.   Enablement may be satisfied so long as someone of skill in the art can make and use the invention based upon the specification without undue experimentation. Information that is common knowledge need not be included. Additionally, product manufacturing specifications do not need to be included. However, sometimes it is difficult to discern the line between adequately enabling use versus product manufacturing specifications.

28. The amount of experimentation necessary, the predictability or unpredictability of the art, the presence or absence of working examples, the nature of invention, the amount of direction or guidance provided, the state of the art, the relative skill of the art, and the breadth of the claims. Although all of these factors are discussed in *In re Wands* (Fed Cir 1988), they will not all be relevant in every case.

29. If an area is unpredictable, inadequate disclosure might result in an undue amount of experimentation for a person of skill in the art to make and use the invention. On the other hand, in a predictable area, less disclosure may be necessary. In general, the areas of chemical and biological arts are considered unpredictable, such that greater detail is required in the specification. For example, because these areas are unpredictable, a claim for the use of a compound in a human may not be adequately supported by data concerning the use of the same compound in a mouse because of great variability in how chemical compounds interact in different organisms. Predictable arts, on the other hand, would typically involve mechanical inventions. So, for example, a claim for a mechanical method of closure may not need to list every variation for someone of skill in the art to know that a button or snap or other similar device would work.

30. **No**. Although 112 speaks of the application being enabled, it is actually analyzed with reference to the claims. In particular, the operative question is whether the application provides enough information to enable someone of skill in the art to make and use the *claimed invention*. Accordingly, without the reference to the claimed invention, it is impossible to evaluate whether the disclosure is adequate.

31. **Yes**. If the rejection is based upon the claims being broader than the specification supports, the enablement objection may be overcome by amending the claims so that they are supported by the actual text of the specification. By modifying only the claims and not the specification, no new matter is introduced.

32. There is no absolute guidepost for evaluating enablement. Both working examples (examples of experiments actually conducted) and prophetic examples (examples that have not been done by the applicant) may provide enablement. However, there is no absolute requirement that either or both be included in every application. Generally, more complex inventions require more examples and likely require more working examples.

[C] Section 112 Disclosure — Best Mode

33. "Best mode" is one of several requirements a patent application must satisfy. It refers to the best mode (or method) that an inventor has of making and using the invention — if he/she has one. Best mode is determined by a two-part test. First, there is the subjective question of whether the inventor possessed a best mode for making and using the invention at the time of the application. If, so, then the second question is an objective one — whether the patent application (or patent) in fact discloses the best mode.

34. Best mode arguably ensures that an applicant not be able to obtain exclusive patent rights without sharing the most important part of the invention. However, some have suggested that the policy ground is weak since the best mode need not be updated after the application, even if one exists. Furthermore, the fact that other countries do not have such a requirement also arguably undercuts the policy basis for having this requirement.

35. **The correct choice is C.** An applicant must disclose the best method of both making and using the claimed invention. The best mode requirement thus is similar to the enablement requirement in requiring disclosure on both how to make and use the invention. **Answers A and B are incorrect** because they only describe part of the requirement. **Answer D is incorrect** because there is no requirement for an applicant to update the best mode once the patent application is filed.

[D] Written Description

36. The requirement ensures that the inventor actually invented the scope of what is claimed. Otherwise, it would be unfair for the inventor to be able to exclude all others from something that he or she had not actually been "in possession of" as of the date of the invention.

37. **The best answer is C. Answer A is incorrect** because although the patent application generally is in writing, that is not the definition of the 112 written description. **Answer B is also incorrect** because written description can actually be a misnomer — in the famous *Vascath* case, the court found that the diagrams from an earlier design application provided an adequate written description for claims in a later utility patent. **Answer D is incorrect** because although an application must conclude with one or more claims, that is not part of the written description requirement.

38. **The best answer is A. B is incorrect** because the specification cannot be amended after the filing date without introducing new matter. **C and D are incorrect** because written description is evaluated based on the application itself. Although some things may be incorporated by reference, these do not include affidavits and papers. Only U.S. patents and patent applications may be utilized.

39. **The best answer is D.** Answers A–D list a possible instance where the PTO might evaluate whether the claim is supported by the written description. The importance of this question is to underscore that the written description requirement needs to be considered not just when the application is filed, but during the entire pendency of the application, since amended or newly introduced claims must still be adequately supported. In addition, where a brand new application claims the benefit of the filing date of an earlier application, the claims of the new application must be compared with the disclosure of the earlier application to see if the written description is satisfied in accordance with 35 U.S.C. 120. There are other requirements necessary to claim entitlement to the filing date of an earlier application, but satisfying written description is definitely one of the core requirements.

[E]   Section 112 ¶ 2 — Definiteness

40.   This paragraph requires that claims be definite. In addition to the requirements in 112 paragraph 1 that the patent provide a written description of the invention and how to make and use it, this paragraph ensures that the claims are adequately clear to give proper notice to the public of the patentee's rights.

41.   **The best answer is B.** The person of skill in the art is the only relevant person through whose eyes claims must be evaluated to see if they are definite. Even if terms seem vague and imprecise to an ordinary observer, they may nonetheless be adequately definite if a person of skill in the art would so find them.

42.   **The best answer is B. Answer A is incorrect** because there is no per se rule declaring certain words always indefinite. Depending on the situation, vague-sounding terms such as "substantially" may still satisfy the definiteness requirement. To evaluate whether the term (and claim) are appropriately definite, a court must consider the claim in light of the specification, as well as the prosecution history from the perspective of a person of ordinary skill in the art. In addition, if there still remains ambiguity, extrinsic evidence to establish the meaning of a term may be relevant, such that **Answer C is also incorrect. Answer D is incorrect** because definiteness is not only a separate requirement of patentability, but also focuses on a different issue. In particular, enablement focuses on whether someone could make and use the claimed invention. In contrast, definiteness focuses on whether the claims are adequately defined so that the public is aware of the full scope of the claimed invention.

[F]   Section 112 ¶ 6 — Means Plus Function Claims

43.   Whereas most claims recite purely structural elements, a claim written in 112 paragraph 6 format may include elements described by their *function*, rather than their structure. The specification is especially important in understanding the scope of such claims since the statute expressly provides that such a claim covers the "corresponding structure, material or acts *described in the specification and equivalents thereof.*"

44.   **The best answer is C. Answer A is incorrect** because while such claims are more typical for mechanical and electrical inventions, the statute does not per se limit them to any class of inventions. **Answer B is incorrect** because there is no rule that only a single element of a claim may be expressed in such manner. As long as there is a claim for a combination, i.e., more than a single element, means plus function language can be used, including multiple functional elements. **Answer D is incorrect** because although such claims are interpreted in light of the specification, the statute expressly states that they cover the corresponding structure and material in the specification and *equivalents*. Accordingly, while close, Answer D is too narrow.

45.   Because means plus function claims are interpreted in light of the specification, rather than in a vacuum, the stated structural elements in the specification serve to provide

adequate definiteness. On the other hand, if the specification failed to provide any corresponding structure, the claim would be indefinite.

[G]   Section 112 Disclosure — Examples

46.   **The best answer is D. Answer A is incorrect** in light of the fact that Answer D is a better answer. In particular, the best mode of practicing the invention of creating artificial skin is not disclosed here since the application omits disclosure of the preferred starting material. However, the enablement requirement is satisfied because someone of skill in the art could make and use the claimed invention, albeit not in the best way. Accordingly, **Answer C is incorrect. Answer B is incorrect** because it falsely states that best mode is adequately disclosed. In addition, written description is not likely a problem based upon the facts provided since the new method is stated to be described in detail.

47.   **The best answer is C. Answer A is incorrect** because Abby is seeking a patent on a product and not a process. **Answer D is incorrect** because it confuses the enablement requirement with best mode; best mode requires more than enabling someone of skill in the art to make the invention. Rather, as part of the bargain with the public for obtaining patent exclusivity, an inventor must disclose the best method of making and using the invention. **Answer B is incorrect** because there is a better answer. In particular, if rubber prepared by Abby's process results in increased yield, but not an improved skin product, that would not need to be disclosed as part of the best mode.

48.   **The best answer is C.** The biggest problem with this claim is that the claim is not enabled for all elements of the fosse class since Judy has not tested the entire class. If undue experimentation is required to assess which members work, the claim is not enabled. Since there is a problem under 112, **Answer A is incorrect. Answers B and D are incorrect** because the claim probably states a sufficiently clear description of the invention for competitors to comport with the requirements of 112, paragraph 2. Written description may be a problem to the extent that the claim is broader than what Judy actually invented since her invention does not cover all elements of the fosse family.

49.   **The best answer is D. Answer A is wrong** because it is only partially correct. In particular, the elements here do provide definiteness to the claim; however, the claim does not provide a written description of what Judy herself invented. There is an additional problem not stated in Answer A, i.e., the claim does not enable one of skill in the art to make and use the invention. Because at least 65% A is required to achieve the desired properties whereas this claim only provides for 10%, the claim is not enabled. **Answer B is incorrect** because it falsely suggests the written description is adequate. **Answer C is incorrect** because it falsely suggests the claim is enabled.

[A]   General

50.   **The best answer is C.** Notwithstanding the fact that 102 begins by stating "a person shall be entitled to a patent unless," the requirements in 102 are not the only ones that must be satisfied to be entitled to a patent. **Answer A is incorrect** because satisfying any one of the criteria under 102 would bar a patent. Moreover, while a patent cannot issue if any of the criteria of 102 exist, those are not the only requirements; for a patent to issue, the invention must also comply with 101, 103, and 112. Accordingly, **Answer B, although better than Answer A, is also incorrect**. In addition, while an application typically aims to show how an invention is novel and nonobvious, there is no requirement that the application explain why each part of 102 is not applicable, so **Answer D is incorrect**.

51.   **The best answer is D.** Every element must exist in the prior art reference for a patent to be barred under 102. The disclosure of a single element is not adequate for 102, so **Answer A is incorrect**. At most, this could be used in combination with other prior art for a showing of obviousness.

Answer C is incorrect because if the prior art reference is a patent, the patent itself must be examined. Whether or not there is a commercial embodiment of the patent is irrelevant if the prior art reference is the patent. On the other hand, a product could theoretically be relevant to a 102 analysis if it was relevant to show that the claimed invention was publicly known or used. However, that is a different consideration. Whatever constitutes the prior art is what should be analyzed for purposes of 102.

Answer B is incorrect because if the prior art is a patent, the entire patent including the specification, is considered for purposes of 102, since the claimed invention is barred if it is disclosed anywhere in the reference. Although the claims are considered part of the patent, the more appropriate reference to use is the entire specification to assess whether all the elements exist. Claims may be relevant to some types of analysis under 102, such as when two different entities assert entitlement for the same invention under 102(g). Although students sometimes find it confusing not to focus on the claims of a prior art patent, it may be helpful to consider a patent as a subset of a printed publication. Most students have no difficulty in considering the entirety of a publication for purposes of analysis under 102(a) or (b). So, just as the abstract of an article (a printed publication) would not be sole basis of examination, so too analysis of a patent is not limited to the claims. Also, it may help to remember that for purposes of 102(a) or 102(b), the goal is to assess whether the claimed invention was previously *described* — and not claimed — in the prior art.

[B]   Date of Invention

52.   **The best answer is B**. The USPTO uses the filing date of the application as the presumptive date of invention. If the USPTO rejects claims based upon prior art before the application filing date, but after the applicant actually reduced the invention to practice, the applicant would then establish an earlier date by affidavit under 37 CFR 1.131. **Answers A, B, and D are incorrect** because they do not describe procedures that are used to establish a date of invention. In particular, the applicant does not need to establish a date of invention, let alone separate dates of conception and reduction to practice in the original application, such that **Answers A and C are incorrect**. Similarly, the USPTO does not challenge the filing date, so **Answer D is incorrect**.

53.   **The best answer is C**. The date of invention is not relevant to 102(b) since the critical time for 102(b) is more than one year before the date of *application*. On the other hand, 102(a) is tied to the date of the *invention*. While the USPTO will presumptively use the application date as the date of invention, an applicant can establish an earlier date to defeat prior art cited under 102(a) with a Section 1.131 affidavit. Because the date of invention is irrelevant for 102(b), **Answers A and B are incorrect**. In addition, although the date of invention is relevant to 102(g), this is not the *only* situation where date of invention is correct. Accordingly, **Answer D is incorrect** as it is not entirely accurate. The date of invention is relevant to both 102(a) and 102(g). However, since none of the Answers list both of these provisions, Answer C is the best answer since Answer D excludes the possibility of 102(a).

[C]   Section 102 Prior Art — Printed Publication

54.   A printed publication is not limited to actual publications. Rather, any written material that is publicly accessible may qualify as a printed publication. As prior art, the publication must sufficiently disclose the claimed invention such that one of skill in the art could make the claimed invention. Whether or not the invention sufficiently discloses the invention is determined based upon whether all elements of the invention are disclosed — either expressly or inherently — such that a person of skill in the art could make the claimed invention. In addition, in determining whether the publication is sufficiently accessible, the relevant test is whether the publication is available to the relevant public. In other words, it need only be relevant to those of skill in the art and not the entire public. In addition, a publication can be deemed "available," even if actual access is somewhat difficult. For example, in the landmark case of *In re Hall*, a court found a PhD thesis that was indexed in a German library to be sufficiently accessible.

55.   **The best answer is D**. The important term here is "publicly accessible," although that term itself requires further elaboration. Although all the other choices come close, Answer D is the best answer because it is the broadest in scope without being overbroad. There is no absolute requirement that a publication be disseminated for it to constitute a "printed publication." Accordingly, **Answers A and B are incorrect**, although Answer B is a slightly better answer in that it recognizes that only the "relevant" public, i.e.,

persons of skill in the art, counts. In addition, while common means of distribution have often included distribution or indexing, these are not the *only* means, such that **Answer C is also correct**. As recently seen in the case *In re Klopfenstein,* a printed publication may also include a presentation that would not be either distributed or indexed. Accordingly, Answer D is the best answer.

56. The court emphasized that the test is a factor-based one and considered the length of time that the display was exhibited, the expertise of the target audience, the expectations that the material displayed would not be copied, and the ease with which the material could have been copied. There was no stated expectation that the information could not be copied and the applicants took no measures to protect the information from copying. In addition, the court deemed that there was no reasonable expectation that displays would not be copied at an academic conference. The invention was relatively simple to understand, leading the court to conclude that only copying a few slides would capture the essence of the invention by the audience, who were clearly people of ordinary skill in the art.

57. **The best answer is D**. Although any document can constitute a printed publication, the problem with the notebook is that storage in an individual's attic is unlikely to be sufficiently accessible to the relevant public. The fact that it is located in the United States does not automatically ensure that it is publicly accessible. All the other choices could constitute printed publications. A published magazine article would definitely be accessible; while most newspaper articles may not constitute printed publications because they discuss inventions only generally, this choice specifically indicates that the article discloses all elements of the invention. **Answer A is incorrect** because it states all elements are disclosed and the Internet is publicly accessible. In addition, while the Russian thesis may not seem very accessible, the Federal Circuit has found a similar situation to be adequate in the case *In re Hall* (German thesis). So, **Answer C is also incorrect**.

58. **None**. What constitutes a printed publication is the same under 102(a) and 102(b) — something written that is reasonably accessible to the relevant public. The distinction lies in the timing of the printed publication that is analyzed. For 102(a), the publication must be available before the "invention," whereas for 102(b), the publication must be available more than one year before the application.

[D] Section 102(a) — Anticipation

59. **No**. An applicant can only be barred a patent under 102(a) by the activity of others. The statute refers to the invention being "known or used *by others* in this country." In addition, it refers to the invention being patented or described in a printed publication "before the invention thereof by the applicant." If the invention is described before the applicant's own invention, someone must have described the invention other than the applicant. In addition, compare and contrast the language in 102(b) which has no

reference to "others." So, where an applicant can bar himself under 102(b), he cannot do so under 102(a).

60. **The best answer is A**. A printed publication constitutes relevant prior art regardless of where it is published. **Answer B is incorrect** because patent-defeating public knowledge or use is limited to activity within the United States. **Answers C and D are incorrect** because they are tied to activity before the date of application, rather than the date of invention. While the date of invention may be identical to the date of application, Answer A remains a better answer. In addition, Answer C is also not correct because the on sale bar only applies to 102(b).

61. **Probably not**. Although anticipation under 102(a) uses the phrase "known or used by others," it is generally understood to require public knowledge or use. Accordingly, if someone invents something, but keeps that knowledge hidden, there is no public knowledge. The classic case is *Gayler v. Wilder* — the second inventor to create a fireproof safe was not anticipated by the earlier inventor because although such a safe was made, its inventive elements (internal construction) were not visible.

62. The reference must describe every element of the claimed invention in adequate detail to enable a person of ordinary skill in the art to make the claimed invention without undue experimentation. The reference need not disclose the precise details of how to make the claimed invention if those would already be known to a person of skill in the art.

63. **The best answer is B**. To be an anticipatory prior art reference, the reference must not only disclose every element of the claimed invention, but also enable one of skill in the art to make the claimed invention. This way, the claimed invention would already be essentially within the public possession, such that the claimed invention would be undeserving of patent protection. However, the anticipatory prior art need only disclose enough information to enable someone of skill in the art to make the claimed invention without "undue experimentation"; in other words, the same "undue experimentation" that is applied to determine whether an invention satisfies 112 requirements is also applied to prior art references. **Answer A is incorrect** because the prior art reference fails to disclose adequate information to enable the invention to be made. In contrast, Answer B specifically notes that the prior art reference discloses enough detail to allow a person of ordinary skill in the art to make the claimed invention without undue experimentation.

However, the disclosure standards for patentable inventions versus anticipatory prior art are not completely identical. In particular, anticipatory prior art need not demonstrate utility, unlike a patentable invention; therefore, **Answer C is incorrect**.

Answer D is incorrect because it is missing a fundamental point — an anticipatory reference must disclose every element of the invention. Although there is some flexibility for how the elements are disclosed (both express and inherent disclosures are possible), there is no flexibility in the requirement that all elements be disclosed. This choice may not reflect a realistic situation, but it is nonetheless not the best choice.

64. **The best answer is A.** Prior art is anticipatory if it contains all elements of the claimed invention, as well as how to make the invention. The prior art here does that. There is no need to identify the utility of ABC since the claim is not limited to the utility. **Answers B, C, and D are incorrect.** Additionally, D is incorrect because obviousness is irrelevant to an analysis of anticipation.

[E]   Inherency

65. **The best answer is C.** All of the answers attempt to describe the strict identity rule for anticipation, i.e., all elements of the claimed invention must exist in the prior art. Answer A is true, but not the *best* answer because C is more precise in recognizing that elements may be disclosed expressly or exist inherently in the prior art reference. **Answer B is incorrect** because anticipation may exist without each element being expressly disclosed. Similarly, **Answer D is incorrect** because while inherency may be relevant to anticipation, there is no need for every element to be inherent.

66. **The best answer is C.** Inherency cannot be established by mere probabilities, so **Answers B and D are incorrect.** In addition, the Federal Circuit held in *Schering v. Geneva* that anticipation by inherency can exist without recognition in the prior art, so **Answer A is incorrect.** Although this decision has been criticized, that is the current state of the law unless and until the Federal Circuit rules otherwise (or, even less likely, the U.S. Supreme Court both accepts certiorari and overrules the Federal Circuit on this issue).

[F]   Genus/Species

67. **The best answer is A. C is incorrect** because it is too narrow; although such issues are common for chemical and biological inventions, they are not limited exclusively to such inventions. **Answers B and D are also incorrect** because they are overbroad — while a genus may anticipate a claimed species, that is not necessarily the case. On the other hand, even if the prior art genus may not entirely anticipate a claim to a species, it may still bar a patent if the claimed species is not obvious over the prior art genus.

68. **The best answer is A. Answer B is incorrect** since anticipation only considers a single prior art reference. **Answer C is incorrect** because either sandals or sneakers both provide all elements of the claim — even if they may do so in different ways, or provide additional elements. **Answer D is incorrect** because so long as a single species is disclosed, the entire genus is anticipated. So, assuming the prior art adequately discloses (and enables how to make) sandals or sneakers, the claim is anticipated.

69. **The best answer is A.** Although not identical to the claimed range, this choice indicates a value (or species) within the claimed range, thus anticipating the entire range. On

the other hand, **Answers B and D are incorrect** because the prior art compounds fall outside the claimed genus. Similarly, although Answer C discloses a similar range, it does not anticipate because the prior art is not a species; therefore, **Answer C is incorrect**. The question would be a closer one if there was an overlap in range.

[G]   Section 102(a) vs. Section 102(b)

70.   **The best answer is C. Answers A and B are incorrect** because the two provisions utilize different time periods as critical dates. **Answer D is incorrect** because the critical date for 102(a) is the date of invention, not the date of application. Granted, it is possible that the date of invention is identical to the date of application. However, Answer C is still more precise, since the date of invention may be earlier than the date of application.

71.   **The best answer is D. Answers A and B are incorrect** because 102(a) is focused on activity before the date of *invention* whereas 102(b) is focused on activity that occurs more than one year prior to the date of the application. **Answer C is incorrect** because an applicant can bar herself under 102(b) since 102(b) includes activities by anyone — including the applicant — that take place more than one year before the filing date.

[H]   Section 102(b) — Statutory Bar

72.   Section 102(b) is intended to encourage applicants to promptly disclose their inventions and thus share them with the public. In addition, it is intended to ensure that inventors do not get an undue extension of a monopoly by using the invention in secret prior to the official patent term. For example, if the invention is on sale to the public for several years before application, the applicant/inventor is arguably already benefiting from commercial exploitation. In such a case, providing a patent could unduly extend commercial benefits. The statutory bar in the U.S. is nonetheless a fairly benign bar since an inventor has a one-year "grace period" to file; during that one year, the inventor may sell the patented invention without loss of any U.S. rights. However, foreign rights will be lost since there is typically an absolute bar if the invention is known at all — whether through a printed publication or use — prior to the date of application.

73.   **The best answer is B.** Although an inventor may bar herself under 102(b), actions of others may also be a bar under 102(b). **Answers A, C, and D are incorrect** because they are each under-inclusive in different ways.

74.   **The best answer is A.** A statutory bar may exist based upon the activity either of the inventor/applicant or a third party. While most statutory bar cases involve activity by the applicant, third-party uses do sometimes occur. Accordingly, **Answer B is incorrect**. **Answer C is incorrect** because experimental use is only relevant to assessing whether an applicant's otherwise patent-defeating use (or sale) may be negated. **Answer D is incorrect** because it incorporates language from the test for public use, but is not relevant to whether activity by a third party may bar a patent.

75. **The best answer is D.** An invention cannot be barred by use in a foreign country under 102(b). On the other hand, use or sale of the patented invention in the U.S. by anyone — including the inventor — will bar a patent. Accordingly, **Answer C is incorrect**. In addition, an invention will also be barred if it was first described in either a patent or a printed publication anywhere in the world, such that **Answers A and B are incorrect**.

[I]   Section 102(b) — Public Use

76. Patent-defeating public use is use of the invention by someone other than the inventor who is not subject to restriction, secrecy, or other limitation. In particular, the focus is the extent of the inventor's control — or lack thereof — over the use of the claimed invention. If the inventor fails to adequately control use of the invention, the inventor loses the right to obtain a patent.

77. **The best answer is B. Answer D is incorrect** because public use requires actual use; mere possibility is inadequate. On the other hand, the use can be of a single person and need not be by a person of skill in the art. Accordingly, **Answers A and C are incorrect**.

78. **The best answer is D.** The use of the device by Fred, as well as by his friends and family, constitutes a public use of the invention. Although public use may be negated if it is "experimental use," the facts here do not support such a finding. In particular, one of the hallmark requirements of experimental use is that the claimed invention remain within the control of the inventor. Here, Fred placed no restrictions on the use of the invention, let alone required any secrecy agreement, and did not seek regular progress reports or feedback. Also, the feedback he was seeking was more for commercial purposes and not to refine the claimed invention. Experimentation after the invention is complete and done solely for commercial purposes is not considered experimental use.

   Answer A is a reasonable choice, but incorrect because Answer D is more complete. It's true that Fred's own use constitutes a public use. However, Answer D explains why he cannot qualify for experimental use. In addition, although Fred's own use counts, use by friends and family would also be considered a public use.

   Answers B and C are incorrect because although they state relevant factors to consider in evaluating whether a use is experimental, they are not the only considerations. Seeking input alone is not adequate. In particular, the more the input is regularized and relevant to the claimed invention, the more value it would have in establishing experimental use. In addition, while lack of payment can be a helpful factor, it is not dispositive. Indeed, experimental use can technically exist even if a patentee has charged money for the invention. Lack of payment tends to support experimental use, but alone is not adequate to establish experimental use.

79. **The best answer is C.** This question focuses on the fact that old compositions do not bar patents on new methods of using old compositions. Although Wygan (or anyone else) cannot obtain a patent on an old product, new methods of using the product are patentable. **Answer A is incorrect** because a new method of using a product is not anticipated by the product itself. The claimed invention is critical in evaluating whether it is anticipated by the prior art. **Answer B is incorrect** because public use also focuses on the claimed invention. Whether or not the product was in public use via its sales as a heart disease drug, those uses do not disqualify the claimed invention for a different use. **Answer D is also incorrect**. In particular, while Wygan did some testing that might possibly be considered public use (although there are actually not enough facts to make this determination), public use is not patent-defeating unless it occurs more than one year before the date of the application. The facts here specifically state that any testing occurred for only six months before the application, so they would not be patent-defeating. As such, experimental use does not even need be considered.

80. **The best answer is C.** This question tests some tricky concepts. First, public use by another party can nonetheless be a bar to the applicant. However, here, the public sale of the beer does not disclose the claimed method. In addition, although the beer was on sale, the claimed *method* was not and could not be discerned from examining the beer. **Answer B is incorrect** because third party activity can in fact bar an applicant from obtaining a patent under 102(b). **Answer A is incorrect** because although a third party's use may be patent-defeating under 102(b), this choice is overbroad. Finally, **Answer D is close**, but confuses the concepts of when the bar comes into effect. In particular, although public use or sale of a product bars a claim to the product, it does not bar a claim to a process that is not disclosed by the product, as in this case.

[J]   Section 102(b) — On Sale Bar

81. **The best answer is C.** The statutory language "on sale" has been interpreted to include both actual sales, as well as offers to sell the claimed invention. However, it does not include assignments of patent rights; selling legal title to the patent is different from selling the claimed invention, i.e., a product or process claimed in the patent. So, **Answers B and D are incorrect**. In addition, **Answer A is incorrect** as unduly limited in scope, since an offer to sell would also invoke the on sale bar.

82. The court looks to see whether an offer to sell is one that is adequately definite to constitute a commercial offer under contract law principles. In addition, the invention subject for sale must be "ready for patenting." An invention may be "ready for patenting" if it is either (1) "actually reduced to practice, or (2) effectively reduced to practice in that there is a description of drawing of the invention from which a person of skill in the art could adequately practice the invention." However, there is no numerical minimum number of sales required to trigger the on sale bar. Furthermore, an invention can be deemed to be on sale and patent-barring even if it is on sale by a third party, i.e., someone other than the applicant or patentee.

83. **The best answer is A.** An invention is "on sale" if it is made available for sale, including both offers to sell as well as completed sales. The completed invention needs merely to be the subject of a commercial offer in the general contract law sense, i.e., one that the other party could accept as a contract. The invention also needs to be "ready for patenting," which is easily satisfied here because she had reduced the invention to practice. **Answer B is incorrect**, but a close second choice. The invention is clearly on sale when the store accepts the offer, but the earliest date that the invention would be on sale would be the date of the offer; therefore, this is not the best answer. **Answer C is incorrect**; since no completed sale is necessary for an invention to be on sale, an actual sale need not be consummated. **Answer D is incorrect** because one of the ways an invention is deemed "ready for patenting" is if it is actually reduced to practice. It may also be shown to be ready for patenting if there are drawings or a description that can enable a person of ordinary skill in the art to practice the invention.

84. **The best answer is C.** The on sale bar has two elements — there is a commercial offer for sale and the invention is ready for patenting. At the time she made the offer and it was accepted, the on sale bar is not relevant because the second part of the test — ready for patenting — is not yet satisfied. So, **Answers A and B are incorrect. Answer D is incorrect** because it is not necessary that the invention be ready when the first offer is made. Rather, the on sale bar may apply if an offer is made and the invention is ready later; however, the relevant date only begins once the invention is ready for patenting.

[K] Section 102(b) and the Relevance of Experimental Use

85. Experimental use is a term for activity that negates what would otherwise constitute patent-defeating activity under 102(b). In particular, experimental use can negate what would otherwise be a public use of an invention, or an invention that is "on sale." However, not any experimentation with the claimed invention will constitute experimental use. Rather, the use must be to actually test the properties of the claimed invention — experimentation to refine a commercial embodiment does not count. In addition, experimental use must be necessary to perfect the invention, such that if the claimed invention is already complete, any further testing would not qualify for experimental use. There is no absolute time that an applicant may experiment under this doctrine; rather, the relevant test is whether the testing was necessary to perfect the invention. So, for example, in *City of Elizabeth,* the court found that a six-year period of testing of a pavement invention was permissible to test the durability. Whether activity is deemed experimental is a fact-intensive inquiry based on the totality of the circumstances, including not only whether testing is necessary to perfect the invention, but also whether the extent of use was reasonable, whether the use was commercial, and whether the invention was within the control of the inventor at all times.

86. **The best answer is B.** Experimental use may negate either public use or on sale bar under 102(b). On the other hand, experimental use is irrelevant to 102(a), so **Answer**

D is incorrect. Answers A and C are incorrect because they are not adequately comprehensive.

87. **The best answer is D. Answer A is incorrect** because the principle of experimental use regarding on-sale bars has no commonality to experimental use defense to infringement — except for the confusing name. In the case of an on-sale bar, experimental use (when shown) negates what would otherwise be a statutory bar to patentability. Even if experimental use negates a statutory bar, this has no bearing on whether a defendant to an infringement claim is entitled to use an invention pursuant to experimental use. In fact, the possibility of so doing is very slim considering the narrow scope of common law experimental use defense. **Answers B and C are both incorrect** because experimental use is not necessary or relevant for activity that is less than one year from the filing date — at such time, the statutory bar has not yet run, so the defense is not necessary.

[L]   Section 102(c) — Abandonment

88. **The best answer is B.** Although there is some overlap with statutory bars under 102(b), 102(c) refers only to abandonment of the right to obtain a patent by virtue of the applicant's own actions. In this way, 102(c) *may* differ from 102(b), since 102(b) can be prompted by actions of someone other than the applicant. Basically, 102(c) reflects similar policy as 102(b), without the same level of detail. Section 102(b) is more frequently used in contemporary practice to reject or invalidate a patent based upon patent-defeating activity of the applicant/inventor.

Section 102(c) is not relevant to whether the applicant can use an invention, so **Answer A is incorrect**; any possible restriction on the applicant's ability to use a patent would be based upon whether the applicant's use infringed the patent of another. While partially correct, **Answer C is ultimately incorrect**, since it incorporates the false premise of Answer A. **Answer D is incorrect** because enforcement of a patent is not governed by any of the provisions of 102; rather, section 102 focuses solely on whether an applicant will be denied a patent. While it is true that enforcement is not possible if a patent is denied, Answer B remains the best answer because it is the most precise.

[M]   Section 102(d) — Foreign Filing Bar

89. 102(d) promotes prompt filing of applications in the United States that claim priority from a foreign application. However, this is not the only thing that would prompt an inventor to file as early as possible. In particular, since an inventor in some cases may use the foreign filing date, rather than the later U.S. filing date pursuant to Section 119, this provision is not the only one that promotes prompt filing.

90. **The best answer is B. Answers A and D are incorrect** because they each state only part of the test for when a patent will be denied under 102(d). Public use outside the U.S. is never relevant, so Answer D is incorrect. In addition, 102(d) focuses only on

foreign applications. Public use is only a type of prior art relevant to sections 102(a) and (b). **Answer C is incorrect** because 102(d) focuses on what was disclosed, rather than claimed, in the prior application.

91.   **The best answer is A. Answers B, C, and D suggest potentially borderline situations**, but A is the best answer because the key part about patent grant with respect to 102(d) is the provision of exclusionary rights. Published patent applications generally do not come with any such rights. On the other hand, Answers B and D both suggest exclusionary rights. In addition, depending on whether rights are provided for an allowed application, Answer C may also indicate a situation where 102(d) bar would be applicable.

92.   **The best answer is D.** The 102(d) bar may be prompted by an application filed abroad by the inventor himself, his legal representatives, or his assignee. Answer B is overbroad and Answer C is under-inclusive — accordingly, **both Answers B and C are incorrect**. **Answer A is incorrect** because 102(d) does provide for some situations where a patent is barred.

93.   **The best answer is C. Answer A is incorrect** since an inventor cannot bar herself under 102(a). **Answer B is incorrect** because 102(b) is inapplicable for an application not yet published. **Answer D is incorrect** because 102(d) bars patentability for inventions that are supported by the earlier-filed foreign patent, even if not expressly claimed.

94.   **The best answer is B. Answer C is incorrect** because there are two situations where the Hungarian application will bar a U.S. patent — under 102(b) (as a printed publication), or under 102(d). **Answer C is too restrictive.** In addition, even if the Hungarian application would not constitute a valid patent, that is not a pertinent inquiry with respect to whether it bars issuance of a U.S. patent under 102(d); accordingly, **Answer A is incorrect. Answer D is incorrect** because while 119 can help establish the benefit of an earlier filing date from a foreign application with respect to anticipating prior art, that does not supersede the bar under 102(d).

[N]   Section 102(e) — Secret Prior Art from an Earlier-Filed Application

95.   This provision bars granting a patent when the claimed invention was previously described in a published U.S. application that was filed before the applicant's invention. 102(e) ensures that a patent is not awarded to someone who was not the first to invent. In particular, even if the second inventor does not have actual knowledge of a prior invention and the prior invention is "secret prior art" that is not available to the second inventor, this rule bars the second inventor from a patent. Note, even though the prior application does not claim the same invention, it can still bar the second application under 102(e). The idea is that if the claimed invention in the second application was actually described in an earlier application, then the second inventor is not the "first to invent," even if he is the first to *claim* the invention.

96.   **The best answer is B**. Even though the prior art reference was not publicly available at the time of its filing, that is the date used for a 102(e) prior art patent application or patent. **Answers A, C and D are thereby incorrect**.

97.   **The best answer is C. Answer A is incorrect** because if the prior application claimed the identical invention, that should be a situation under 102(g), not 102(e). **Answer B is incorrect** because no actual patent needs to issue to bar the applicant's patent. **Answer D is incorrect** because the 102(e)(1) bar is contingent on the prior published application being filed before the applicant's *date of invention* and not merely the applicant's filing date.

98.   **The best answer is B. Answers A and D are incorrect** because 102(e) is limited to prior descriptions, and not claims of the same invention. **Answer C is incorrect** because although PCT applications may create a bar under 102(e)(2), only PCT applications that designate the United States and are published in English establish such a bar — accordingly, Answer C is overbroad.

99.   **The best answer is A**. An applicant will be denied a patent for an invention that is described in a previously filed U.S. application that has been published. There is no requirement under 102(e) that the published application issue as a patent to be prior art, so **Answer B is incorrect**. In addition, 102(e) applies regardless of the citizenship of the prior applicant, so **Answer C is incorrect. Answer D is incorrect** because if the applications claimed the same invention, that is not a problem under 102(e), but, rather, possibly under 102(g).

100. **The best answer is C**. The facts here describe patent-defeating prior art under 102(e). This is a prototypical case of "secret" prior art that the applicant could not have had actual knowledge about prior to applying. However, the statute nonetheless considers prior U.S. applications that subsequently publish to be prior art. **Answer A is incorrect** because actual knowledge is irrelevant to 102. In addition, 102(e) is designed to cover prior art that applicants likely have no actual knowledge. **Answer B is incorrect** because 102(e) permits U.S. applications to be prior art from the date they are filed and not the date that they are actually published with respect to subsequent applications. **Answer D is incorrect** because 102(e) is a bar if a prior application *discloses* the claimed invention. It is irrelevant whether the prior application has similar claims.

[O]   Section 102(f) — Derivation

101. Section 102(f) prohibits granting a patent to someone who derived an invention from another — for example, 102(f) prevents granting a patent to someone who was told of another's conception. To invalidate a patent based upon 102(f), the challenger must show that the alleged inventor actually acquired knowledge of the claimed invention from another, or that the claimed invention would have been obvious to one of ordinary skill in the art based upon knowledge acquired from another. This provision is not intended to bar a patent to someone who independently invented the same invention.

102. Vicki is probably not barred by 102(f) since the article was only the inspiration for her invention and she needed to do further experimentation, as well as modification, before achieving her invention. If the entire conception of her invention was communicated in the article, however, that would pose a problem.

103. **The best answer is C**. Derivation under 102(f) may be established without regard to the place from which it was derived. The only important element is that the invention was previously conceived by another, as corroborated through testimony and/or documentation. Although this might still be a challenge for Britney, it is the best option.

    Answers A and B are incorrect because invalidity under 102(a) or (b) must be based upon a "printed publication," patent, or public knowledge *within the United States*. Here, there is at most public knowledge or use, but it is not within the United States, so it does not qualify as prior art under 102(a) or (b).

    Answer D is incorrect because 102(e) must be based upon a prior application or patent (with additional requirements) and there is no such application or patent here.

[P] Section 102(g)

104. **The best answer is C**. Although 102(g) does not provide all the rules governing interferences, 102(g)(1) does establish a situation for barring patentability in interference-only contexts. 102(g)(2), on the other hand, applies to all contexts outside interferences. In other words, any application may be potentially barred a patent under 102(g)(2). **Answers A and B are incorrect** because only one provision of 102(g) is limited to the interference context. **Answer D is incorrect** because it reverses the correct rule as stated in Answer C.

105. There are two stages of an invention. The first is the mental conception of the invention. The reduction to practice is the second step. Reduction to practice can be "actual," such as a working model. Or, it can be "constructive," if a patent application is filed. In that case, even if there is no working model, reduction to practice is constructive because a patent application by definition must sufficiently disclose and enable another person of skill in the art to practice the claimed invention.

106. Reasonable diligence refers to the fact that an inventor was continuously active in working toward a reduction to practice of a conceived invention, or that a legitimate excuse exists for any period of inactivity. Diligence is only relevant in proceedings under 271(g) where an inventor was first to conceive, but last to reduce to practice. In that case, the first inventor must be reasonably diligent from the time immediately prior to the second inventor's conception. Notably, the first inventor need not be diligent from his/her initial conception.

107. Reasonable diligence only applies when an inventor is first to conceive, but second to reduce to practice. If the inventor is first to conceive and reduce to practice, that inventor easily wins the patent.

108. **The best answer is E**. Reasonable diligence is only relevant to 102(g) situations where the first to conceive is also last to invent. If the first person to conceive is also the first to invent, that person "wins" an interference proceeding, so **Answer A is incorrect**. **Answer C is incorrect** because prior creation of an invention in a WTO country is only applicable to interferences and not to 102(g)(2) defenses.

109. Proof of invention must be corroborated by another under 102(g). This can be done by a live witness, or through documentation that is witnessed.

110. **The best answer is D**. Although the inventors' actions are clearly relevant, a patent may be barred by activity beyond the inventor's actions, such that Answer A is too narrow. Similarly, although an assignee's actions may be relevant, an invention may be barred due to activity of the inventor as well, such that Answer C is similarly too narrow. Answer B correctly notes that the inventor and the corporate assignee's actions are both relevant, but is ultimately not the best answer. D is the most precise in noting that the actions of the patent department in particular are also relevant.

111. **The best answer is A**. Although other answers may seem promising, A is the only completely correct statement. However, this is a tricky question because there are presumptions and inferences that can arise. In particular, if there is a "long" passage of time between reduction to practice and filing of an application, that can raise the *inference* of concealment. **Answer B is incorrect** however because it states that this establishes concealment. **Answer C is incorrect** because courts have imputed delay by a corporate assignee to the inventor, even when the inventor has no control over the actions of the corporate assignee; in particular, delays by a corporate patent department in timely filing an application are imputed to the inventor. In addition, although inferences of concealment that may arise due to long delay may be rebutted by perfecting an invention, the only type of perfecting that is relevant is perfecting of the *claimed* invention and not perfecting of commercial aspects, so **Answer D is incorrect**.

[Q] Section 102(g)(2)

112. Section 102(g)(2) is a bar to patentability that can be applied just as 102(a), (b), (c), etc. Accordingly, 102(g)(2) can be raised either by the USPTO, or by a defendant in a litigation. **Answers A and B are incorrect** because each situation described would be appropriate to raise 102(g)(2). On the other hand, 102(g)(2) is not relevant to inferences, so **Answer C is the best answer**. There is a similar, yet different, provision related to inferences — 102(g)(1). **Answer D is incorrect** because only one answer is true.

113. **The best answer is C. Answer A is incorrect** because 102(g)(2) only refers to activities by someone other than the inventor himself. In this sense, it has some commonality with 102(a). **Answer B is incorrect** because 102(g)(2) is limited to activity within the United States. The only patent-defeating activities beyond the U.S. that are considered

are printed publications and patents. **Answer D is close, but ultimately incorrect** since creation by someone in a WTO country is applicable to interferences under 102(g)(1), but not 102(g)(2).

[R]   Interference

114.   An interference proceeding is designed to determine who was first to invent. It is not relevant in countries where a patent is awarded to the first person to file an application. However, the term "first to invent" can be a bit misleading since the actual statutory provision is more complicated.

115.   **The best answer is B.** An interference is subject to the jurisdiction of the USPTO, so a district court is not involved; **Answer A is incorrect**. In addition, although the U.S. is a "first to file" system, this does not mean that every patent examination requires evaluation of whether there is any other competing application for the same invention. Rather, an interference is the only type of situation where the USPTO assesses which application was first to invent. So, **Answer C is incorrect**. While partially correct, **Answer D is not the best answer**, since interferences are not limited to U.S. citizens or residents. There is, however, a limitation to proof of inventive activity — in particular, evidence of inventive activity is limited to countries that are members of NAFTA or WTO; however, since WTO includes most countries of the world, this is not much of a limitation.

116.   **The best answer is A.** An interference can only be declared with at least one pending application. An interference may be declared between two patent applications, or an application and a patent. However, an interference may never be declared between two patents, even if they do have overlapping subject matter. Accordingly, Answer A is correct in describing a situation where an interference may not be declared, and **Answers B-D are incorrect**.

117.   If an invention would be obvious, there is no need to provide a patent and doing so
        would result in a monopoly on something that was previously available, or at least could
        have been available to those of skill in the art.

118.   **Yes.** Although the Federal Circuit has long held that "obvious to try" is not relevant
        to assessing obviousness, the Supreme Court recently resurrected this theory as relevant
        in *KSR v. Teleflex.* While the *Graham* factor analysis is still the appropriate analytical
        framework, *KSR* clearly indicates that "obvious to try" may in fact be relevant to a
        103 analysis.

119.   **Answer C is the best answer**, since it reflects the three-step test set forth by *Graham*,
        as reinforced by *KSR v Teleflex..* Although none of the choices here mention secondary
        considerations of nonobviousness, this may also be a relevant consideration.

        Answer A is incorrect because the flash-of-genius test that was once espoused by the
        Supreme Court has been replaced with the three-step *Graham* analysis. **Answer B is
        incorrect** because it is incomplete. While it is true that something more than the skill
        of a mechanic is typically required for a nonobvious invention, this does not encompass
        the complete standard. **Answer D is incorrect** because only one statement is true.

120.   Generally, the same types of prior art references under 102 may be used to evaluate
        whether an invention is obvious under 103. Section 103 does not set forth new types
        of prior art. Accordingly, the same prior art, i.e., printed publications, patents, public
        use or sale (within the U.S.), etc., may all be used for assessing obviousness. The major
        distinction is that whereas all elements of the claimed invention must appear in a *single*
        reference for a 102 bar, elements may be used from multiple references, or a single
        reference together with what is known to someone of skill in the art. However, whether
        an obviousness analysis may be based upon 102(c) abandonment, or 102(d) foreign filed
        application is more ambiguous — *Oddzon* has dicta suggesting that this is improper,
        but *Kathwala* suggests that this is appropriate. Similarly, although 102(f) derivation and
        102(g) prior invention by another may be combined with 103, there are certain limits
        based upon 103(c) concerning common ownership of subject matter.

121.   There is no set number of references required. An invention may be deemed obvious
        based on a single reference. If only a single reference is used, the distinction between
        102 anticipation and obviousness is that for anticipation, all elements of the claimed
        invention must exist (expressly or inherently) in the prior art whereas the claimed
        invention may be obvious based upon a reference that discloses most, but not all
        elements of the claimed invention.

122.   **The best answer is C.** Although obviousness rejection usually involves multiple references, even a single reference may suffice. The key difference between 102 versus 103 is that a single reference must describe every element of an invention. Where a single reference describes all but one element, that reference may be combined with either another reference, or knowledge of a person of ordinary skill to establish the obviousness of the claimed invention.

   Answer A is incorrect because there is not set number of prior art references that must be considered for a 103 rejection. **Answer B is incorrect** because if a reference disclosed every element of the claim, it should be rejected for anticipation under 102, rather than obviousness. **Answer D is incorrect** because a claimed invention cannot be found obvious based upon any references without regard to whether they are *pertinent* references to the problem to be solved. Unlike 102(a), Section 103 limits the scope of references relevant to analysts to those that are "pertinent."

123.   **Yes.** An inventor is assumed to have knowledge of all relevant prior art (*Winslow's Tableau*). Accordingly, whether or not the inventor had actual knowledge is irrelevant to determining whether a claimed invention is obvious. This is similar to analysis of anticipation under 102 — an invention may be barred under 102 or 103 based upon prior art that the inventor had no actual knowledge. The idea is that the public does not benefit from granting a patent to an inventor for something that was actually in the prior art, or would have been easily created from the prior art because it was obvious. There is no reason to provide someone with the reward of a patent simply because they were unaware of what was actually publicly available.

124.   **Yes,** an invention may be found obvious based upon prior art that is from a different technological endeavor if that prior art would have been considered reasonably pertinent to the problem being solved to a person of reasonable skill in the art. Essentially, there are two classes of prior art references that are relevant to an obviousness analysis: either prior art from the same endeavor, or prior art from a different endeavor that would nonetheless have been pertinent to the problem being solved by a person of ordinary skill. In other words, is the prior art from the same area of invention, or an area that the inventor should have consulted for the problem? These two categories together comprise what is referred to as "analogous prior art" that may be properly used for 103 analyses. This is an important distinction from what type of prior art is used for 102 anticipation; in particular, a claimed invention may be anticipated by prior art from *any field* of endeavor so long as it contains all the elements of the claimed invention. However, although stating these two categories may be simple, assessing when something is in the same field of endeavor or pertinent to the problem being solved may be sometimes a matter of interpretation. Unlike anticipation analyses, there is room for subjectivity within an analysis for obviousness. Determining what constitutes analogous art is actually just one issue in which subjectivity may play a role.

125.   **The best answer is C.** Whereas there is no restriction on the field of invention that may be used for 102, only analogous art may be used for consideration in 103 analyses.

Answer A is incorrect, although somewhat of a red herring. In particular, while the same general *categories* of prior art are used, i.e., patents and printed publications, these constitute legitimate types of prior art for both 102 and 103. However, in responding to the question at hand, there is a difference in the types of prior art used. If Answer A were examined on its own, it would be tempting. However, Answer C is a better answer.

Answer D is incorrect — at least in part. It correctly states that prior art for 102 includes all fields of technology. However, neither 102 or 103 are restricted to what an inventor has actual knowledge of. The relevant standard is one based upon reasonableness with regard to a person of ordinary skill in the art.

Answer B is incorrect, although also partially correct. In particular, while prior art under 103 is limited in scope, it is not limited solely to the relevant field of endeavor; it may also include other areas of technology that would be pertinent to the problem being solved. In addition, B is also incorrect since there is no restriction on the type of prior art that may be utilized for 102.

126. **The best answer is A**. Although obviousness may be evaluated at different times (including during the application process, as well as during an infringement suit), the only relevant reference time for assessing the scope and content of the prior art is the time the invention was made. Whenever the question of obviousness is raised, the inquiry focuses on whether the claimed invention would have been obvious at the date of invention. Accordingly, **Answers B, C, and D are incorrect**.

127. **Maybe**. Public use is a relevant type of prior art under both 102(a) or 102(b), so that is not a problem. Even if the prior art does not use the same material as Donna claims, it may nonetheless be relevant for a 103 analysis. In addition, if a person of ordinary skill in the art of can-cooling inventions would have known to substitute Donna's material for foam, Donna could be facing a 103 rejection.

128. **The best answer is A**. Although Eva did not anticipate Donna's invention, her suggestion could be a problem as 102(f) prior art combined with 103. In particular, if based upon Eva's disclosure, a person of ordinary skill in the art would have easily combined Eva's idea with the other elements of her invention that would be a problem for Donna.

Answers B and C are incorrect, although only slight variations of these choices would have made these legitimate answers as well. First, both choices involve analogous prior art. In addition, both Answers B and C are based upon 102(e) prior art based upon "secret prior art" that is not known to the applicant at the time of filing. **Answer B is incorrect** because patent applications filed before an applicant under 102(e) can only be used if they are published. **Answer C is incorrect** because although granted patents that issue after an applicant's filing date are permissible under 102(e), the patent must be a U.S. patent, or an international application that designates the United States and is published in English. These are some tricky distinctions to 102(e).

Answer D is incorrect because although it discloses a relevant type of prior art, it is not analogous art. This prior art is attempting to keep something warm, rather than cool. In addition, the manner in which this patent addresses the temperature issue is totally different in not using something surrounding the cup. A very broad interpretation of the field of invention as encompassing preserving the temperature of a beverage could possibly include this as an analogous invention. But, given that Answer A exists, that is a better answer.

129.   There are a number of factors that may be considered in assessing the level of ordinary skill in the art — not all of which must exist in every case. In particular, a court may consider the typical education level required for the type of technology, including how sophisticated the technology is. For example, in some cases, a court has considered that the person of ordinary skill would be a hobbyist, such that no higher education is necessary. In addition, a court may consider the types of problems encountered in the technology, as well as how quickly innovation occurs.

130.   The TSM test was created by the Federal Circuit as a method to guard against hindsight bias in examining whether an invention was obvious. According to the test, references could not be combined unless there was a teaching, suggestion, or motivation in the prior art to combine the reference. Although the test could consider whether someone of skill in the art would be motivated to modify prior art to achieve the claimed invention, or whether the problem to be solved inherently suggested a change, the test was widely criticized for resulting in too many "bad" patents. This criticism led, in part, to the Supreme Court decision of *KSR v. Teleflex*. The Supreme Court has not expressly disavowed the use of the test, but did indicate that an inflexible application was erroneous. For example, the Court clarified that motivations may be implicit based upon the knowledge and skill of a person of ordinary art. In addition, motivation may arise from market pressures and design needs. In addition, the motivation of the inventor/patentee is not relevant — rather, the focus is on the person of ordinary skill and whether they would find a particular combination of elements and/or references to be obvious.

131.   Although there is no express suggestion, *KSR* now informs us that obviousness need not be applied rigidly. While elements from disparate field of technology should not be combined, obviousness can consider whether a person of ordinary skill in the art would be motivated to combine elements from analogous art. To assess whether the invention is obviousness, the court would need to determine the level of skill in the area and whether someone with such skill would have been motivated to make the combination. The fact that the invention is a combination invention will not alone preclude patentability since almost all inventions are combinations of pre-existing elements. However, if design needs motivated combination of elements, that could suggest that Barry's invention is obvious.

132.   Secondary considerations are objective factors based on how the invention performs, rather than solely based on its technical merits, although secondary considerations are only properly considered for 103 if they have a nexus with the claimed features of the

invention. Typical factors, such as failure of others, long-felt need, commercial success, and widespread licensing include considerations beyond the basic *Graham* framework that may be considered in evaluating whether an invention is obvious. Only if secondary factors have a *nexus* to the claimed invention may they be considered in establishing obviousness; the nexus is essential. On the question of whether secondary considerations must always be considered, the Supreme Court has stated that they may be considered, whereas the Federal Circuit in *Hybritech* stated that secondary considerations must always be considered, such that failure to do so is reversible error. Although the U.S. Supreme Court recently addressed the issue of obviousness in *KSR* and did affirm that secondary considerations were relevant to the consideration, the issue of whether failure to consider such factors was reversible error was not before the court and not addressed. Accordingly, unless and until *Hybritech* is expressly overruled, district courts should be considering secondary considerations of nonobviousness.

133. **The best answer is B.** Although no single statement provides the complete test for obviousness, Answer B is the most correct statement since secondary considerations are only relevant where they supplement — not supplant — the other parts of the *Graham* test. A proper obviousness analysis would first begin by asking who is a person of ordinary skill in the art, then consider the scope and content of the prior art, followed by the differences between the prior art and the claimed invention. The secondary considerations may additionally be used, but they do not supplant the rest of the analysis, so **Answer C is incorrect**. In addition, **Answer D is also incorrect** because the proper analysis always begins with a focus on the person of ordinary skill and a comparison of the prior art to the claimed invention.

Answer A is incorrect for two reasons. First, it fails to indicate that a nexus between the claimed invention and the secondary considerations is necessary for them to be relevant. In addition, it is also incorrect because it is not necessary for a majority of those considerations to exist to establish nonobviousness.

134. Commercial success could be attributable to other factors, such as market dominance, or strength of advertising, rather than whether the invention is a substantial improvement over prior art. Similarly, licensing might not have a nexus to the claimed invention if licensees feared litigation.

135. **The best answer is A** because if a patent owner has no market dominance, the commercial sales and licensing are more likely attributable to the claimed invention itself. **Answers B and C are incorrect** because although they cite secondary considerations — commercial success and widespread licensing — there is no indication that such considerations have any nexus to the claimed invention. Accordingly, **Answer D is incorrect** because not all statements are true.

136. Prior art under these categories may not bar a patent if the prior art and the claimed invention were both owned (or subject to assignment) by the same person at the time the claimed invention was made. Ownership or assignment can be established if the

invention was subject of a joint research agreement that was effective at the time the invention was made, the claimed invention was a result of activities within the scope of the agreement, and the application for the claimed invention discloses (or is amended to disclose) the names of parties to the agreement. The full details of this exclusion from obviousness are set forth in 103(c) and were intended to recognize the realities of modern research where inventions may be created by multiple inventors, including inventors that technically work for different entities.

[A] General

137. **The best answer is D**. An earlier filing date means that prior art filed between the earlier filing date and the actual application is not counted against the applicant. However, there is a potential downside for applicants in using an earlier date since it means that the patent term may be shorter than if they used the actual date of filing. In particular, since the patent term is calculated from the earliest effective date, claiming an earlier date for purposes of prior art also results to a shorter term. Prior to 1996, claiming an earlier effective date had no negative repercussions on the patent term since the term was a fixed period of seventeen years from date of issuance.

Answers A and B are incorrect because examination of applications is not a function of an earlier filing dates. Applications are examined roughly in the order in which they are received, i.e., the actual filing dates, regardless of whether an earlier filing date is claimed according to sections 119 or 120 of the Patent Act. In addition, Answer A incorrectly states that the earlier filing date is not relevant to calculating the filing date. This is false since the same date is used both with regard to comparing the claimed invention to the prior art, as well as for calculating the patent term of 20 years from the earliest effective filing date.

Answer C is incorrect because although it accurately notes that the earlier filing date is used for examining prior art, it fails to recognize that the same date is used for assessing the patent term.

138. A claim is entitled to an earlier filing date only if it is supported by the disclosure of an earlier application filed by at least one similar inventor. In other words, an applicant can only claim an earlier filing date if the earlier application actually disclosed the later-claimed invention such that the later-claimed invention can be considered to have been filed at the earlier time for prior art purposes.

[B] Earlier Effective Date — U.S. Application (Section 120)

139. **The best answer is D**. There is no requirement of a common assignee to benefit from an earlier filing date under 120. On the other hand, Answers A–C all list requirements that must exist for an application to claim the benefit of an earlier filing date. **Answer A is incorrect** because it accurately states there must be at least one inventor in common between the two applications (although additional inventors are permitted). **Answer B is also incorrect** because it accurately states the earlier application must be co-pending when the second application is filed, claiming the benefit of the earlier date. Although

the earlier application may later be abandoned, or subject to issuance, the copendency requirement must be satisfied at the time the earlier filing date is sought. **Answer C is also incorrect** because it accurately states the second application must include a specific reference to the earlier filed application from which it is claiming the earlier date. This can either be done in the initial application, or the application can be amended to include this reference after the original filing.

140.   **The best answer is B**. Applications are considered "co-pending" as long as both are actual applications with the PTO at the time the second application is filed. Abandonment of the first application after the second application has been filed is consistent with claiming an earlier filing date under Section 120.

  Answer A is incorrect because the first application does not exist at the time of filing of the second application; an issued patent is no longer pending before the PTO as an application. **Answer C is similarly incorrect** because if the first application is abandoned prior to when the second application is filed, there can be no co-pending applications. **Answer D is incorrect** because there is a correct answer.

141.   **The best answer is C**. To be entitled to the benefit of the earlier filing date of a prior U.S. application in accordance with 35 U.S.C. 120, there are several requirements that need to be satisfied. First, there needs to be at least one inventor in common; this requirement is easily met here, since Joe is an inventor on both applications. Second the applications must both be pending at the time the second application is filed; this is also explicitly stated as true. Third, the second application must also contain a specific reference to the first, which the facts do indicate. Last, but not least, the specification of the first application must support the claims of the second application with respect to satisfying all the requirements of 112 such that it is fair to engage in the fiction that the second application was actually filed at the time of the first one. After all, if the claims are supported by the first application, that means that they could have been filed at the time of the first application.

  Answer A is close, but incorrect. While it is true that the specifications are identical, the relevant requirement is that the specification of the first *supports* the claims of the second. Even if the specifications are identical, if the claims in the second application are overly broad, they will not be entitled to the earlier filing date.

  Answer B is incorrect because there is no need to use the actual filing date here where the requirements of Section 120 are satisfied. In addition, support from an earlier specification is irrelevant if the earlier filing date is not used.

  Answer D is incorrect since only one inventor needs to be in common — identical inventors are not required unless there is a single inventor on the earlier application.

142.   **The best answer is D**. This question is a bit tricky because it requires you to recall several different aspects of patent law. First, it is true that a claim will be anticipated if every element is disclosed in the prior art; however, what counts as prior art is a

function of the date of invention. The PTO assumes that the filing date is the date of invention, although there are two situations where an applicant can claim an earlier date. First, an applicant may establish through a 1.131 affidavit an earlier date that the invention was actually reduced to practice to overcome a 102(a) prior art reference. **Answer C is incorrect** because it states that this is the *only* method. In particular, an applicant can also rely upon an earlier date for purposes of prior art if the applicant is entitled to claim the benefit of the earlier filing date of an application according to Section 120 (prior U.S. application) or Section 119 (prior foreign application) of the Patent Act. **Answer B is incorrect** because 102(b) requires that the prior art exist more than one year before the date of the application and that does not exist here. **Answer A is closer, but ultimately incorrect**, because there are certain instances where an applicant may overcome prior art published before the date of invention. While the PTO may issue a rejection using the actual filing date as the date of invention, that assumption may be overcome.

As was already mentioned, Answer C is incorrect, but a better answer than A, since it recognizes one way in which an applicant may overcome an anticipation rejection. Answer C suggests that an applicant can file a 1.131 affidavit to establish a date of invention earlier than the presumptive date of invention, i.e., the actual filing date. While this is a method that is often used to overcome 102(a) rejections, it is not the best answer here because it is not the *only* situation in which prior art before the actual filing date is not counted against the applicant. Although Answer D only includes one option, it does not suggest that this is the only option available to the applicant and hence is a better answer. However, in both situations, the PTO is allowing the applicant to provide evidence to overcome the presumptive date of invention based on the filing date.

143. **The best answer is C.** The issue here is whether each claim is adequately supported by the disclosure of the parent application, such that it is entitled to use the earlier filing date. If so, then the intervening prior art is not deemed anticipatory. **Answer B is incorrect** because it assumes that all claims in the CIP are entitled to the earlier filing date. The issue is whether the parent application supports claims to both compound X as well as any solid material. Since the parent application contains no disclosure for material other than compound X, the parent cannot support any claims broader than compound X; so Jill's first claim is not entitled to an earlier filing date. **Answer D is incorrect**. In addition, **Answer A is incorrect** because the second claim is not anticipated when the filing date of the parent application is used, as is appropriate here. The two applications were co-pending at the time the second application was filed, there was a common inventor, and the second claim is supported by the disclosure of the earlier application.

[C] Earlier Effective Filing Date — Foreign Application (Section 119)

144. **The best answer is C.** The principal distinction between applications claiming an effective filing date under 119 as opposed to 120 is that the parent application is not from the United States. The citizenship of the applicant is not relevant; **Answer A is**

incorrect. In addition, although this section focuses on applications filed outside the U.S., not all such applications are considered. **Answer B is overbroad** because Section 119 only permits priority claims when the parent application is filed in a country that provides "similar privileges" to applications filed in the U.S., or to U.S. citizens, or in a WTO member country. **Answer D is also incorrect** because it is overbroad.

145.   **The best answer is B.** There is no copendency requirement for priority under 119; that is only an issue for priority stemming from a U.S. application under 120. Copendency applies only to applications pending before the same office — a situation that would never exist if the earlier application was foreign filed, so **Answer A is incorrect. Answer D is incorrect** because there is no requirement that the same individual apply for the first and second application. In fact, in many countries, assignees can and do file patent applications in their own name (rather than the inventor's), such that it would often be impossible for identical identities of applicants. There is a requirement that the second application be filed within twelve months in accordance with the Paris Convention. The important time period is twelve months from the *earliest* date, not the latest. So, **Answer C is incorrect**.

146.   **The best answer is C. Answer A** is incorrect because Section 119 has no nationality requirement for applicants. **Answers B and D are incorrect** because Section 119 only permits claiming priority when the U.S. application is filed within 12 months of the *earliest* foreign application. In this case, Claudia waited too long to assert priority. She can still file in the U.S., but any intervening art that came into existence after February 2, 2005, may defeat her application. She could have avoided this situation by filing the U.S. application by February 1, 2006.

147.   **The best answer is D**. The issue here is whether Frank is entitled to the benefit of the earlier filing date in Japan under 35 U.S.C 119. To be so entitled, the foreign country must provide the same privileges to U.S. citizens, or be a WTO member country. Here the facts tell you that Japan is a WTO member country, so the first requirement is satisfied. In addition, the U.S. application must be filed within twelve months from the earliest corresponding foreign application. Since the earliest (and only) foreign application is filed on March 12, 2006 and the U.S. application is filed March 1, 2007, the U.S. application is timely field. Frank's application must also include a specific reference to the Japanese application, including the specific application number and filing date during the pendency of his U.S. application. However, assuming that is satisfied, he should be entitled to the earlier date.

       Answer A is incorrect because an inventor cannot bar himself under 102(a). **Answer C is incorrect** because whether an earlier application is co-pending is only relevant to claiming an earlier filing date of a U.S. application, not of foreign applications. **Answer B is incorrect** because although a patent application is a type of prior art that may create a statutory bar, Frank can claim an effective filing date of March 19, 2006 to avoid the prior art. Note, while it is true that the Japanese application must be published to constitute 102(b) prior art, the bigger issue here is that even if published,

Frank will not be barred because he is entitled to the benefit of the earlier filing date. Accordingly, Answer D is the best answer.

148. **The best answer is D. Answer A is incorrect** because a statutory bar only exists if there has been more than a year since a printed publication became available; that does not exist here. A 102(b) bar reference would need to be available before March 1, 2006 (one year before the actual U.S. filing date) — the January 2007 publication of the Japanese application is definitely too late. **Answer B is close, but not the best answer** — while it is true that the Japanese application discloses the same invention and is not barred under 102(b), this answer does not explain whether Frank will be able to claim an earlier filing date with respect to other prior art. **Answer C is incorrect** because it wrongly suggests that Frank cannot claim earlier priority under Section 119 because the claimed inventions are different. Although tricky, the rule is that so long as the claimed invention in the U.S. application was fully disclosed in the earlier application, the two inventions are considered "the same" with respect to being able to claim the benefit of an earlier filing date in accordance with Section 119.

149. **The best answer is C.** The issue here is what filing date an applicant may be entitled to where there is more than one corresponding prior foreign application. Section 119 of the Patent Act allows an applicant to claim the benefit of an earlier filing date from a foreign application if the U.S. application is filed within one year. However, the one year is from the *earliest* corresponding application. In this case, the earliest application would be March 12, 2006. So, Frank had to file his U.S. application by March 12, 2007 to be entitled to the earlier date. It does not matter that he filed another foreign application with a later date. **Answer B is incorrect** because the latest foreign filing date is irrelevant for purposes of 119. That would defeat the purpose of encouraging applicants to promptly file their applications in the U.S. The important issue to remember where there are multiple foreign applications is that the priority date is calculated from the *earliest* foreign application. **Answer A is incorrect** because although this is the date that would generally be used for a 119 priority claim, Frank fails to satisfy the 119 requirement of filing the U.S. application within one year. **Answer D is incorrect** because an applicant has no opportunity to choose a date under 119. There is only one possible date (March 12, 2006 here) and only if the applicant timely files within one year.

150. **The best answer is D**, since all of the listed situations are ones where inventorship would be relevant. Since each joint owner of a patent (which joint inventors presumptively are) is entitled to make, use, offer to sell, or sell the patented invention without the consent of the other owner, a license from one owner would be a valid defense against an infringement suit by the other owner.

151. **The best answer is D**. Section 116 of the Patent Act expressly states that joint inventors may apply together for a patent "even though (1) they did not physically work together or at the same time, (2) each did not make the same type or amount of contribution, or (3) each did not make a contribution to the subject matter of every claim of the patent." **Answers A–C are incorrect** in light of the statutory text, even if some of the statements may seem logical based upon the common use of the word "joint" outside the patent context. Also of note is that the current statute has been in effect since 1984; older cases may espouse a heightened standard for joint inventorship.

152. **The best answer is D**. Although possibly counterintuitive from a "labor perspective" of patent rights, the current state of law permits each joint inventor rights to the entirety of the patented invention. **Answer A is incorrect** because each joint inventor has rights to the entire patent and not just the claim(s) he or she contributed to. Similarly, **Answer B is incorrect** because each joint inventor as a co-owner of a patent may grant licenses without consent of the others. **Answer C is close, but ultimately incorrect** because no accounting is necessary to other joint inventors (in contrast to joint authors under copyright laws).

153. **The best answer is D**. While section 116 states that all inventors must file jointly for an application, there are separate provisions that expressly provide for correction of inventorship in issued patents under section 256, such that **Answer A is not the best answer. Answer B is incorrect** because reexamination is limited to questions of patentability based upon prior art. **Answer C is incorrect** because section 256 permits either the USPTO or "the court before which such matter is called in question" to evaluate the inventorship issue. One critical issue in correcting inventorship is whether the problem was the result of deceptive intent on the part of the nonjoined inventor.

154. **The best answer is D**. Correction of inventorship is done by a different provision than other types of corrections. **Answer B is incorrect** because it confuses the timing of requesting (broadening) reissue applications with correction of inventions. **Answers A and C are incorrect** because the relevant statute, section 256, allows correction by the USPTO, as well as any court.

[A]   Patent Rights — Scope of Rights

155.   **The best answer is D.** This answer most closely mirrors the statutory text of 35 U.S.C 271(a). The patentee also has the additional right to exclude others from importing the invention into the United States. **Answer C is incorrect** because although the patentee may exclude others from making and using the invention, this choice is less comprehensive than Answer D. **Answers A and B are incorrect** because they confuse the right to *exclude* with an affirmative right to make and use. The patentee has no fundamental right to make or use an invention and may in fact need a license from another patent owner; however, Answer B does correctly state that the patentee has the right to exclude others from importing the invention into the United States.

156.   **The best answer is D.** A patent owner has the right to *exclude* others from his invention, but not an affirmative right to make or use his own invention. Although patent owners can often use their invention, they may sometimes need to get a license from another patent owner. This is especially true if Bob's patent is for an improvement — while Bob may be entitled to a patent for an invention that is new and nonobvious, this does not mean that his machine does not fall within the scope of broader claims. For example, if a prior patent claimed all radar detectors, Bob would infringe.

   Answers A and B are incorrect because they confuse the right to exclude with an affirmative right to make and/or use. **Answer C is incorrect** for similar reasons, since a patent does not grant a right to use. In addition, patent rights would not trump all state laws. It is possible that a patent is granted for an invention that may not be used because of other laws, whether federal or state. For example, if use of a radar detector by those other than law enforcement is illegal in certain states, its patented status still does not permit use.

[B]   Infringement — Analytical Steps

157.   The court must first construe the claims and then apply the construed claims to the accused device or method. Only if every element of the properly construed claim is found in the accused device or method (either literally or by the doctrine of equivalents) may infringement exist.

158.   **The best answer is C.** The basic two-step process to analyze infringement consists of first construing the claims and then comparing the properly construed claims to the accused device. Until the claims are properly construed, they should not be compared to the accused product, such that **Answer B is incorrect**. In addition, the only relevant

product to an infringement analysis is the accused product of the defendant; the patentee's product — if any — is not relevant to an infringement analysis. Accordingly, **Answer A is incorrect**. Similarly, whether or not the defendant has a patent covering its accused product is not relevant to an infringement analysis, such that **Answer D is incorrect**. A patent is not a defense to infringement and is also not part of an infringement analysis.

[C]   Claim Construction

159. **Yes**. Although ordinary meanings are considered, the entire context of claims, including other claims, claim differentiation, and the specification and prosecution history, are relevant. The specification of one patent may define a claim term in one patent that is completely undefined, or even different than the meaning given to it in a different patent. The facts of every case are critical to claim construction.

160. Extrinsic evidence is always permissible to provide background concerning the technology of the invention, but should not generally be consulted unless and until the intrinsic evidence (claims and specification and prosecution history) has been consulted without any clear results.

161. Claims are to be construed from the perspective of a person having ordinary skill in the art. A dictionary or other reference may indicate what a term means to such persons. Alternatively, a witness may testify to what people of skill in the art would commonly understand a term to mean. Patents, including claims, are intended to be public documents that are understood to a person of ordinary skill in the art. The claims are to be interpreted without regard to what an inventor later alleges he intended them to mean. Statements in the specification and prosecution history from the inventor, however, would be relevant.

162. **The best answer is B**. Although there has been a great deal of confusion in the Federal Circuit jurisprudence concerning claim construction, the Federal Circuit case law now firmly holds that claim construction may *not* begin with dictionary definitions, making **Answer C is incorrect**. **Answer D is also incorrect** because the literal language of the claim is the starting point, so that extrinsic evidence, including expert testimony, should not be. As a general matter, extrinsic evidence is not appropriate for consideration unless and until all the intrinsic evidence (such as claims, specification, and file wrapper) has been consulted and nonetheless yields an unclear answer. **Answer A is close, but not the best answer** because, if the claims alone, or the claims and specification together, adequately define terms, the file history may not be necessary. Furthermore, Answer A fails to differentiate the appropriate order.

163. The general principle of claim differentiation is that where there is a dependent claim, the independent claim from which the dependent claim derives is assumed not to include the limitations in the dependent claim.

164. **The best answer is B. Answer A is incorrect** because the appropriate perspective is that of the person of ordinary skill in the art, rather than that of an ordinary lay person. **Answer C is incorrect**, although a tricky principle to apply in practice. Basically, claims should be interpreted *in light of* the specification but should not be limited to the examples in the specification; the distinction between the two is often a fine line in practice. **Answer D is incorrect** because although claim construction always begins with the plain meaning of the claims, the specification and even the file wrapper must typically be consulted. Answer D is also incorrect because dictionary definitions and other extrinsic evidence should not be consulted until all the intrinsic evidence has been consulted without a clear answer. The Federal Circuit at one point seemed to resort to dictionary definitions first, but this is no longer the current practice.

165. **The best answer is B**. Claim construction is a question of law according to the U.S. Supreme Court. *Markman v. Westview*. **Answers C and D are incorrect** because they miss this issue. In addition, while the issue of patent infringement may involve factual questions, the first step of the infringement analysis — claim construction — still only involves a question of law. **Answer A is incorrect** because claim construction does not necessarily occur before discovery. The timing of claim construction is typically determined by the district court and/or local rules. While some local rules require early claim construction, many others have no rules at all.

[D]   Patent Infringement — General

166. **The best answer is B. Answer A is incorrect** because the term "comprising" permits infringement to exist if additional elements beyond those explicitly claimed are included. **Answer C is incorrect** because "substantially identical" is not a pertinent test to patent infringement (although it may be relevant to other types of intellectual property infringement, such as copyright). **Answer D is incorrect** because literal infringement requires every element of the claim to exist in the accused device, but one element is missing here. The function of the widget overall is not relevant to literal infringement. Moreover, even for infringement under the doctrine of equivalents, the analysis for equivalence is based on an individual element and not on the entirety of the product.

167. **The best answer is A**. Because the claim uses the word "consisting," an infringing widget must consist of the exact elements, i.e., A, B, and C. If the claim had used "comprising," infringement could exist if additional elements existed, but because "consisting" was used, **Answer B is incorrect. Answers C and D are incorrect** because infringement requires that every element exist in the accused device, either literally or via the doctrine of equivalents. Although one way to determine the doctrine of equivalents is to consider whether elements of a claim have the same function and perform in the same way with the same result, **Answer C does not accurately state this test**. Moreover, the doctrine of equivalents looks for an equivalent to a missing element and not to the overall object. In this case, whether the overall widgets are equivalent is not a pertinent question; if there is only literal infringement of A and B, infringement can only exist if the equivalent of C exists, but there is no such information

here. **Answer D is incorrect** because it erroneously evaluates whether the widget overall is equivalent; furthermore, it completely disregards the elements of the claim, which is impermissible for any type of infringement analysis.

[E] Doctrine of Equivalents

168. The doctrine is intended as an equitable measure to prevent unscrupulous infringers from avoiding liability because of a simple substitution or other insubstantial change that is essentially equivalent to the literal scope of a claim. However, because the doctrine introduces uncertainty with respect to the notice function of claims, the doctrine must balance uncertainty against appropriate incentives and rewards to inventors. These differing issues provide some basis for understanding why courts may want to limit the doctrine substantially without eliminating it entirely.

169. **The best answer is B.** For considering the equivalence of claim elements under the doctrine of equivalents, there is no temporal limitation to what is known at the time of application. Such a limitation is only relevant to infringement of means plus function claims. **Answer C is incorrect** because any narrowing amendment made for patentability reasons — including, but not limited to prior art — may give rise to a presumption of estoppel. **Answer A is incorrect** because the doctrine of equivalents applies to individual elements of a claimed invention and not to the invention as a whole. **Answer D is incorrect** because although modifications to a patent application may raise a presumption that equivalents are barred, it is a rebuttable presumption, such that there is no absolute bar.

170   **The best answer is C. Answer A is incorrect** because while Joe does not literally infringe, this does not mean that he cannot infringe under the doctrine of equivalents. **Answer B is incorrect** because the doctrine of equivalents is used only for individual elements of a claim where literal infringement does not exist; it is not used to compare the overall claimed composition. **Answer D is incorrect** because it is an overbroad statement concerning when a patentee is estopped from using the doctrine of equivalents. The doctrine does not provide an absolute bar.

172. A patentee should not be entitled to gain through the equitable doctrine that he could not have obtained initially. For example, if a patentee narrowed a claim to overcome cited prior art, the patentee should not be able to broaden the literal scope of the claim to recover what was explicitly disavowed. In addition, because patents, together with the prosecution history, are public documents that are intended to give notice to competitors, it would be unfair to permit a patentee to enlarge claims where the prosecution history would suggest that the claims could not so be enlarged.

The patentee may be limited in using the doctrine of equivalents to establish elements that lack literal infringement if the patentee had previously narrowed the claims for a reason relating to patentability. Reasons relating to patentability are not limited to prior art; amendments to address Section 112 rejections may also serve to limit use of the doctrine. The patentee is presumed to disclaim what is given up when claims are narrowed, even if the amendment is made without any clear reason relating to patentability. In addition, even if the claim is not narrowed, the doctrine of equivalents may not be used to encompass what would have been unpatentable in light of the prior art. Furthermore, even if there is no clear evidence that a claim was narrowed for reasons of patentability (i.e., claims are amended without explanation), a court will presume that this was the case, subject to limited rebuttal by the patentee.

173. **The best answer is C**, although this question is a bit tricky regarding some difficult material. **Answer A is incorrect** because although it expresses the general idea, it is overbroad in suggesting that inventor testimony during litigation is adequate. Rather, to establish that a patentee had no intent to surrender equivalents, the Federal Circuit has established specific situations as guidelines. **Answer B is close, but ultimately incorrect** because reliance on inventor testimony during litigation is not adequate to rebut the presumption. It is true that a patentee may rebut the presumption by showing tangentialness, but must do so based solely on the intrinsic evidence, i.e., the prosecution history, without the introduction of any additional evidence, except perhaps evidence from those necessary to establish how one of skill in the art would interpret the intrinsic evidence. **Answer D is also close, but still incorrect**. In particular, one way a patentee may rebut the presumption is if there were "some other reason" suggesting a patentee could not reasonably have been able to describe the insubstantial equivalent in question. Although this factor is broadly stated, the Federal Circuit has indicated that it is actually a narrow test which includes at least the shortcomings of language. Answer D is ultimately incorrect because although intrinsic evidence should be the primary source, there is no complete bar to using extrinsic evidence as necessary to show knowledge of a person of skill in the art.

[F] Infringement — Examples

174. Whether Nogo infringes should not be assessed based solely on the literal claim. Although the words of the claim are the starting point for analysis of infringement, the first step is to construe the claims. Depending on how the claim is construed, Nogo might infringe literally without any need to even consider the doctrine of equivalents. In particular, if the specification gives any indication that there should be room to broaden the range of the numerical limits, that would be relevant.

175. **The best answer is D**. Literal infringement can only exist if the defendant's device falls within all elements of the patented invention. The question expressly states this does not happen here. In addition, infringement under the doctrine of equivalents requires more than similarity of the overall product, so that **Answer A is incorrect**. In particular, the accused product must satisfy every element of the claimed invention either literally or under the doctrine of equivalents. Since there is no information to suggest that this exists here, B is not liable. **Answer B is incorrect** because secondary infringement requires direct infringement by someone, but none appears in the question. **Answer C is incorrect** because, although B arguably could be considered to have derived the

general idea for his yo-yo from A's patent, derivation is only an issue with respect to patentability for B. Derivation can bar a patent under 102(f), but is not an affirmative cause of action.

176. **Answer C is the correct answer. Answer A is incorrect** because intent is irrelevant to direct infringement; it is only relevant to secondary infringement (i.e., inducement or contributory infringement). **Answer D is incorrect** because infringement is not dependent on whether a defendant is entitled to its own patent. Rather, the pertinent analysis is simply whether the defendant's activities fall within the scope of the claim. **Answer B is incorrect** because how a product appears to a consumer is not relevant to infringement. In addition, infringement under the doctrine of equivalents can only exist if there is an insubstantial difference, or if the element in the defendant's product performs the same function in the same manner and in the same way as the equivalent element of the patented invention.

177. In practice, a defendant may often be sued under both provisions. Section 271(c) is narrower, since the statutory provision has a number of elements that must be satisfied. For example, liability can only ensue for someone who makes a material component of a patented invention that is not a "staple" article of commerce and is not suitable for any substantial use other than for the patented invention. Section 271(b) is about inducing infringement. Intent is very important, but provision of a part of the patented invention is not necessary.

178. Direct patent infringement is a strict liability offense such that intent is never relevant. However, secondary infringement under 271(b) and (c) does look at the intent of the actor. Intent may also be relevant to liability under 271(f) by supply of components of a patented product to a location outside the United States.

179. **The best answer is D**. Although patent liability is sometimes analogized to tort principles, the topics do not entirely intersect. In particular, whereas tort liability may allow intent to cause one action to establish liability for a different cause of action, liability for inducing patent infringement requires intent to actually induce patent infringement, and not merely intent to cause action that happens to constitute infringement. Knowledge of a patent and what constitutes infringement are both important.

Answer A is incorrect because inducement cannot exist without actual knowledge of the patent. **Answer B is incorrect** because inducement cannot exist without direct infringement by someone. A guilty conscience alone is not adequate for inducement. **Answer C is close, but not correct** because although knowledge of a patent is required, the action taken to induce infringement only counts for inducement if it is done during the patent term. So, even if there is knowledge of a pending patent application and action is purposefully taken before the patent issues to induce literal infringement during the actual term of the patent, there is no cause of action against the person who prematurely induces the literal infringement.

180. **The best answer is A**. Making a component that is a material part of the invention is not enough to create liability for contributory infringement — even if that component has no substantial noninfringing use. While all of the choices use terminology from 271(c), the key to this question is that the relevant activity for contributory infringement liability is offering to sell, selling, or importing the component. Mere manufacture of a component is not adequate. Similarly, although not a choice here, mere use of a component would also not be enough. **Answers B–D are incorrect** because they all state situations where contributory infringement would exist.

181. If someone sells a component that is not useful for anything other than infringing, it can be inferred that the individual was attempting to induce infringement. Where liability is predicated on acts that are less than the complete invention, the level of intent is heightened. Also, this element helps courts to ensure that liability does not ensue when there are legitimate alternative uses to a component. In addition, if a component is a staple article of commerce, consumers should not be deprived from non-infringing uses.

182. **The best answer is A. Answers B–D are incorrect**, as they all describe a situation where a component is not a staple article because it seems to only be useful for infringement. Iron, on the other hand, is a staple article used in many products.

183. **The best answer is C.** Stan does not literally infringe because he has not made the complete invention, i.e., an assembled shopping cart. However, he could potentially be liable for a type of secondary infringement. For example, if Stan knows about Bob's patent and intentionally induces his customers to infringe by providing them with instructions on how to complete Bob's invention, he could be liable. Similarly, Stan could be liable for contributory infringement if the components he sells have no substantial noninfringing use. However, if the unassembled pieces he sells are easily used as standard-sized construction materials, or some other substantial (as opposed to throw-away) function, it is possible that Stan would not be liable for contributory infringement because the pieces could constitute a staple article.

      Answer A is incorrect because it unduly limits liability to direct infringement. It is true that Stan does not directly infringe, but there are other possible ways to infringe. **Answer B is incorrect** because while direct infringement may exist either through literal or doctrine of equivalents analysis, all elements of the claimed invention must be present and there is no evidence of that here. **Answer D is close, but not correct** because secondary infringement can never exist without direct infringement by another actor.

184. **The best answer is A.** If the components offered by Stan have no substantial noninfringing use, i.e., their only use is to create Bob's shopping cart, then Stan would be liable. **Answer B is incorrect** because inducement cannot exist without knowledge of the patent. **Answer C is incorrect** because it mixes the requirements of inducement and contributory infringement. For inducement to exist, it is irrelevant whether there is sale of components without substantial noninfringing use. Rather, inducement exists if there is knowledge of the patent and actual inducement of activity that constitutes infringement, knowing that such activity constitutes infringement. **Answer D is incorrect** because while the statutory language establishes liability based on sale of a single component, there is no reason why sale of all of the components of the patented invention cannot result in contribution unless the components constitute staple articles.

185. **The best answer is C. Answer A is incorrect** because while Lisa will not be liable for direct infringement, she may be liable for contributory infringement. **Answer B is incorrect** because offers for sale of a material part of the invention provide a basis for contributory infringement as well as actual sales. **Answer D is incorrect** because

if no one uses Lisa's apparatus according to the patent, there is no direct infringement, and thus no predicate for contributory infringement.

186. **The best answer is D. Answer A is incorrect** because inducement cannot exist without knowledge of the patent; also, inducement cannot exist without direct infringement. **Answer B is incorrect** because actual direct infringement is required. **Answer C is incorrect** because whether or not she sells a material part of the invention is only relevant to contributory infringement and not inducement.

187. **The best answer is B**. This question focuses on the issue of patent exhaustion or first sale. Basically, the patentee exhausts its rights in a product upon the first sale. So, if GM was licensed to make the patented convertible top, the patentee has no right to bring an action against anyone who buys a car from GM. A valid purchaser is entitled to dispose of the patented item as they wish; accordingly, **Answer A is incorrect. Answer C is incorrect** because the patent rights have been exhausted, although it is generally true that lack of knowledge is not a defense to direct infringement. **Answer D is also incorrect** because it ignores the patent exhaustion rule and also had no basis for contributory infringement which requires providing a material part of the patented product and not the entire patented product.

188. **The best answer is C. Answer A is incorrect** because infringement can only exist if all elements of the invention exist. **Answer B is incorrect** because indirect infringement requires more than an intent to avoid infringement. Some type of scienter, or intent, is relevant, but not a mere intent to avoid infringement. **Answer D is incorrect** because infringement under 271(g) is only relevant for patented methods under certain circumstances.

189. In each case, liability involves intent, as well as a component of the patented invention that is not a staple product capable of substantial noninfringing use. Contributory infringement under 271(c) exists if someone sells, offers for sale, or imports a component of a patented invention. Liability under 271(f), on the other hand, exists if someone supplies a component of a patented invention from within the United States to someone outside the United States. In addition, in both cases there must be assembly of the patented invention; however, in the case of 271(f), the activity occurs outside the United States.

190. **The best answer is D. Answer A is incorrect** because although importation of a patented process results in infringement, it is infringement under 271(a) (direct infringement and not 271(g)). Liability under 271(g) is about activity that does not fall under the standard infringement provision of 271(a). **Answer B is incorrect** because while closer, it is too broad. Liability does not exist for importing any product of a patented process. Rather, there are specific limitations under (g)(1) and (g)(2) that are reflected in Answer D. **Answer C is incorrect** because although the statute was enacted in response to concerns and lobbying by the biotechnology industry, the statute does limit its application to this type of technology.

191. **The best answer is C.** The standard term of a patent is 20 years from the earliest effective filing date. This may be the same date as the actual filing date of the patent application. However, in the many cases where patent applicants claim an earlier date for purposes of prior art under Section 119 or 120, an earlier date is used. Accordingly, **Answer B is incorrect.** In addition, while patent term used to be calculated from issuance date prior to amendments to comply with WTO/TRIPS, that is not applicable for applications filed on or after June 8, 1995. So, **Answers A and B are incorrect. Answer D is also incorrect.**

192. **The best answer is A** since this is the date that is 20 years from the earliest effective filing date. **Answer B is incorrect** because it calculates the term from the date of the non-provisional application, rather than the effective filing date. **Answers C and D are incorrect** because they are based on the date of patent issuance, which is no longer relevant to calculating patent terms.

193. **The best answer is A.** Although the claims of CIP applications are evaluated differently with reference to prior art, depending on whether the claim is supported by the original or the CIP application, no such distinction is made for the patent term. Accordingly, **Answer C is incorrect.** Also, **Answer B is incorrect** since the patent term is calculated from the earliest effective filing date, and not the actual application date. **Answer D is incorrect** because the date of patent issuance is not relevant here.

194. **The best answer is B.** The patent term is twenty years from filing, which means twenty years from February 1, 1997, i.e., February 1, 2017. The patent will have expired after that time, such that **Answers C and D are incorrect.** In addition, **A is incorrect** since there is no infringement under 271(a) before a patent issues. The only possible liability for activity that occurs before a patent issues is under Section 154(d) (provisional rights) when the published application claims are substantially identical to the issued claims and the defendant had knowledge of the published application. However, this is not applicable here, as the answer only specified 271(a).

195. A patent term may be extended if the issuance is delayed by failures of the USPTO to timely examine the application, as well as for delays due to interferences, secrecy orders, and appeals. In addition, for a limited category of inventions, the patent term may be "restored" for part of the time lost when a patent is filed on an invention subject to approval of the FDA that is necessary before it can be sold to the public. To "restore" patent term lost, an applicant must submit an application to the USPTO in accordance with Section 156.

196. **Yes**. If the mistake was made "in good faith," this would seem an appropriate error for a certificate of correction since a typo satisfies the statutory requirement that the error be of "a clerical or typographical nature, or of minor character."

197. **The best answer is A**. Adding new information is not permissible with a certification of correction, such that **Answers B, C, and D are incorrect**. Furthermore, Answers B and D describe actions that are not appropriate at any time during prosecution unless a CIP is filed. Narrower claims also may result after reissue.

198. **No**. Although this situation seems to satisfy the "good faith" requirement for the mistake, a certificate of correction is not permissible when the proposed change would alter the scope of the patent claims. However, if a reissue application is filed, the error could be corrected.

199. **No**. Although Abby has some of the relevant requirements for reissuance (such as lack of deceptive intent and possibly an inoperative or invalid patent if it does not meet 112), she cannot seek reissue here. The statute specifically provides that "no new matter shall be introduced" and the drawing here would constitute "new matter" since it was not included in the original application.

200. **No**. Although reissue proceedings allow applicants to broaden (or narrow) claims, they may only do so if the patent is at least partly inoperative or invalid. In this case, although she wants to broaden her claims, there is no indication that her current patent is inoperative or invalid.

201. **Probably not**. Reissue is only proper if the patent is *invalid* — not just because the patent fails to capture all possible infringement. In addition, Cassie may not be able to satisfy the requirement that an "error" in claim scope occurred without deceptive intent.

202. **The best answer is D**. Although there is a two-year time limit, this is only applicable to applications to broaden the claims, so that **Answers A, B, and C are incorrect**.

203. **The best answer is C**. The basic rule is that a reissue application is one that is "broadening" if *any* aspect of the claim is broadened — even if part of the claim is simultaneously narrowed. Accordingly, **Answers A, B, and D are incorrect**. Also, for a reissue application that attempts to broaden a claim, the reissue must be filed within two years of the original patent grant.

204. **The best answer is D**. If a patent is reissued, the term of the patent is the same as the original patent. So, **Answer C is incorrect**. In addition, as part of a reissue

application, the original patent must be surrendered. Accordingly, if the reissue application is rejected, no patent exists, so **Answers A and B are incorrect**.

205. **Yes**, but only if the claims are "substantially identical" to the claims of the original patent.

206. **The best answer is D**. A third party that makes a product outside the scope of the original patent claims is not later liable for activity that was not infringing under the original patent. In particular, the third party can continue to make and use the product that was not infringing under the original patent. However, *after the reissue patent is granted*, whether the third party can continue to make products that are now infringing is a closer question. The statute provides that the court *may* provide for "continued manufacture, use, offer for sale or sale" of a product for which "substantial preparation" was made prior to the reissue grant. Accordingly, whether Fred can *continue* to make new devices will depend on whether a court finds that he had made substantial preparation previous to the reissue grant.

207. In both cases, the rule bars the applicant/patentee from inconsistency. In evaluating infringement, a patentee is entitled to use DOE to broaden claims slightly beyond their literal scope, but prosecution history estoppel bars the patentee from trying to broaden claims to recapture what was previously given up intentionally. Similarly, in a reissue application proceeding, a patentee/applicant cannot attempt to use reissuance to claim subject matter previously surrendered to overcome a prior art rejection.

208. Anyone can seek a reexamination of any claim of a patent at any time — even including the Director of the USPTO. Unlike reissue applications, reexamination requests are not limited to the patentee.

209. Due to a legislative overruling of *In re Portola Packing*, in all reexamination applications since 2002, a substantial new question of patentability may be based upon patents or printed publications that were previously considered by the PTO.

210. **The best answer is A**. Reexamination must be based on a substantial new question of patentability based on prior art consisting of patents and printed publications; whether or not the PTO has previously considered the reference is irrelevant. **Answers B, C, and D are incorrect** because they relate to patentability issues that are not permissible for consideration in reexamination.

211. **The best answer is B.** "Any person" may request a re-examination, including the Director of the PTO. Accordingly, **Answer C is incorrect**. Examinations of reissue applications may consider any basis of patentability that makes the patent inoperative; on the other hand, reexaminations may only consider 102 and 103 issues based on printed publications and patents. So, **Answer D is incorrect**. In addition, claims may only be broadened in a reissue proceeding, so **Answer A is incorrect**.

212. **The best answer is C.** The patent is presumed valid. Although that may be challenged by the defendant, there is no need for the plaintiff to affirmatively prove validity in the first instance, such that **Answers A and B are incorrect.** Rather, the plaintiff's burden is only to establish that the defendant's accused product or process infringes at least one claim of the patent. In addition, **Answers B and D are incorrect** because the defendant has the burden of establishing any possible defenses.

213. **The best answer is B.** A patent is presumed valid pursuant to 35 U.S.C. 282. In addition, although the defendant may rebut the validity, he can only do so with clear and convincing evidence. **Answers C and D are incorrect** because a patent has a presumption of validity. **A is incorrect** because proof beyond a reasonable doubt is a standard applicable to criminal cases, but need not be met for patent cases.

214. **The best answer is C** because any condition for patentability is a proper defense to patent infringement.

 Answers A and B are incorrect because they are inconsistent with 35 U.S.C 282. The validity of each patent claim is considered independent of other claims. In addition, dependent claims are presumed valid even though dependent upon an invalid claim.

 Answer D is incorrect because an invalid patent may not be asserted against other parties. The doctrine of mutuality (requiring identical parties to exist in both cases as a pre-requisite to preclusion) has been rejected for patent infringement cases.

215. **The best answer is E.** Any requirement of patentability may be asserted as a complete defense to patent infringement, so that **Answers A and B are both correct.** In addition, if an invention is repaired, rather than reconstructed, that is also a proper defense. Finally, unenforceability is also a complete defense to a patent that is valid and infringed.

216. **The best answer is C.** Common law experimental use is a very limited defense. **Answer B is incorrect** because *Madey v. Duke* clarified that use of a patented invention in an academic institution is not necessarily immune from infringement. **Answer D is incorrect** because infringement is not avoided simply because a corporation does not yet have a specific commercial product. The scope of common law experimental use is limited to when a defendant makes or uses the claimed invention purely for idle curiosity.

 A is incorrect because independent invention is not a general defense to patent infringement since knowledge is not a requirement of patent infringement.

217. **The best answer is C.** This question focuses on the fact that although there is no per se statute of limitations to asserting patent infringement claims, there is a time limitation on recovery of damages under 35 U.S.C 286. In particular, this provision states that "except as otherwise provided by law, no recovery shall be had for any infringement committed more than six years prior to the filing of the complaint or counterclaim for infringement. . . ."

    Answer A is incorrect because there is technically no statute of limitations. Although there is a limitation on the scope of recovery, there is no bar to bringing patent infringement actions. **Answer B is incorrect** because when the patent owner first becomes aware of infringing activity is not relevant. Even if the patent owner had no knowledge of the infringing activity, the owner is still precluded from damages for any time longer than six years prior to a suit for infringement. **Answer D is incorrect** because although there is a limitation on recovery of damages, there is no complete bar to monetary damages. Rather, the limitation is only on the number of years for which damages are available — the patent owner may recover for six years prior to the complaint, but no more. Although Tom may possibly obtain an injunction, D is still incorrect because of the erroneous statement concerning damages.

218. **The best answer is B.** The doctrine of laches is intended to limit recovery of damages for a plaintiff that unreasonably and inexcusably delays the initiation of an infringement action, such that the defendant is materially prejudiced. The patentee is not entirely barred from recovery, but is barred from obtaining damages for the period before the suit was initiated.

    Answer A is incorrect because although it does note that unreasonable delay by the patent owner is relevant, it erroneously states that the patent owner is completely barred from asserting a claim.

    Answer C is incorrect because the doctrine of equitable estoppel is a complete defense that entirely bars a claim for infringement. In particular, where the plaintiff misleads the defendant into reasonably believing that the plaintiff does not intend to enforce its patent, the defendant relies on the plaintiff's actions and is thus materially prejudiced, equitable estoppel will exist.

    Answer D is incorrect because it is overbroad. While it is true that laches and equitable estoppel are both defenses to infringement, they do not both bar recovery from damages. Also, it is somewhat imprecise with respect to equitable estoppel since a plaintiff patent owner's suit is entirely precluded if the equitable estoppel is shown. Laches is a more limited defense since it only minimizes some recovery of damages.

219. A "repair" of a patented item is a permissible, but a "reconstruction" is considering an infringement (making the patented invention). Accordingly, in a patent infringement litigation, if a defendant is able to establish that it was repairing the patented item, that would be a complete defense. The issue typically arises where the patented item has

been legally purchased, but then subsequently modified. Generally, a patent owner's rights are exhausted by the first legal sale of a patented item; the purchaser has an implied license to not only use the patented device, but also to repair it. Theoretically, reconstruction involves more extensive creation of the device, such that the activity is considered analogous to making the patented device. However, what constitutes permissible repair versus impermissible reconstruction can be difficult to discern. The inquiry is a fact-intensive one. Some relevant factors include whether the part that is repaired was intended to expire before the entirety of the patented device, whether the patentee intended repair of the part, and whether there is a market in replacing the spent part. *Sandvik Aktiebolag v. E.J. Co.*, 121 F.3d 669, 43 U.S.PQ2d 1620 (Fed. Cir. 1997),

220. **Probably not**. Practical necessity is not a defense to patent infringement. In addition, experimental use does not exempt all scientific research. Experimental use that falls within the common law defense only qualifies when it is done for "idle curiosity." The facts here seem more similar to the situation in *Duke v. Madey*, where the Federal Circuit found that because the university was in the business of securing grants, research conducted at the university was not exempted under the doctrine of experimental use.

221. Invalidity refers to whether a specific claim is invalid. Since each claim is evaluated separately, invalidity is a limited defense if a patent owner asserts multiple claims. Unenforceability, on the other hand, renders the entire patent — every claim — unenforceable.

222. **The best answer is C**. Inequitable conduct may be based upon three types of conduct. The most typical is failure to disclose material information. However, inequitable conduct also exists where there is submission of false information relevant to patentability, as well as affirmative misrepresentations material to patentability. Accordingly, **Answer A is incorrect** as being unduly limited in scope. A recent case involving affirmative misrepresentations is *Purdue v. Endo*, where the patentee suggested clinical significance, but actually had no scientific proof for its assertions. Although subsequent research ultimately held the patentee's predictions to be accurate, the court still found the patent invalid for inequitable conduct because of the intentional misrepresentation. **Answer B is incorrect** because inequitable conduct is only a defense that may be asserted during litigation proceedings. Even if the conduct is known at the time of re-examination and is based upon failure to disclose prior art, inequitable conduct is not within the scope of re-examination. **Answer D is incorrect** because inequitable conduct always requires an intent to deceive. A court may balance the level of materiality against the intent to deceive, but intent is nonetheless required.

223. A patent owner is entitled to compensatory damages, prejudgment interest and costs. In addition, the patent owner *may* also be entitled to an injunction and attorney fees.

224. **The best answer is B.** There are no statutory damages for patent infringement, unlike copyright law, so **Answer A is incorrect.** A tougher choice is between C and D. The statute provides that in no circumstance will a patentee recover less than a reasonable royalty. It is possible that a patent owner may obtain lost profits, but additional proof of causation is required and it is not guaranteed, so **Answer C is not correct. Answer D is incorrect** because the statute refers to a reasonable royalty as a floor for damages, such that lost profits could never be provided if lower than a reasonable royalty.

225. Amma should focus on the equities of the situation since there is no absolute entitlement to preliminary injunction; rather, it is subject to the equitable discretion of the district court. The patentee must minimally show a reasonable likelihood of success on the merits to be granted a preliminary injunction. So, if Amma can make a strong showing that the patent is invalid, there would be no such reasonable likelihood of success. Moreover, if Amma is the only producer of a medical product, an injunction would seem inconsistent with public health policies.

226. **The best answer is C.** The U.S. Supreme Court recently held in *eBay v. MercExchange, LLC*, that a court must apply the traditional four-factor test for preliminary injunctions in patent cases. A court must consider all factors, including the balance of hardships to both sides. Financial hardship that may accrue to the defendant because of a preliminary injunction is not dispositive; a court may find after weighing all the factors, that an injunction and resulting financial hardship are appropriate. **Answer A is incorrect** because there is no automatic presumption of likelihood of success on the merits in a patent case. Rather, a patentee must show a reasonable probability of success on the merits for infringement, as well as validity and enforceability. If a patentee can do so, the court will probably presume that there is irreparable harm. However, **Answer B is incorrect** since courts will not assume irreparable harm in every case regardless of whether the patentee is likely to succeed. **Answer D is incorrect** because public interest must be considered from the perspective of patent owner as well as the public. While the patent owner may have an interest in enforcing its patent, the public interest may weigh in favor of the infringer if the infringer is the only supplier of a public necessity, such as a medical device.

227. **The best answer is D.** 35 U.S.C. 285 provides for attorney fees in exceptional cases. For example, the Federal Circuit has found "exceptional" circumstances to include willful infringement, inequitable conduct, and filing frivolous suits. **Answer A is**

incorrect because there is no requirement that the patent owner must actually use the invention. There are no statutory damages for patent infringement, so **Answer C is incorrect**. In addition, although patent law does provide for the possibility of treble damages, the statute the statute only permits courts to do so and does not mandate such a result; accordingly, **Answer B is incorrect**.

228. **The best answer is D** because attorney fees may be predicated on a number of factors. **Answers A–C are all possible factors** that could provide a basis for attorney fees.

229. The reasonable royalty is calculated based on a number of assumptions. In particular, the court attempts to assess what the parties would have agreed upon as reasonable business parties prior to the first infringement. This is admittedly not only a hypothetical negotiation, but also a fictional one. Nonetheless, that is the general framework set forth in *Georgia Pacific* and courts have subsequently provided a number of factors to consider. For example, some factors include the patent owner's licensing rates to others, and industry rates of licensing in a given area of technology.

230. When damages are based on "lost profits" rather than "reasonable royalty," the court attempts to assess what profits the patentee has lost. The patentee is not entitled to all of the defendant's profits because there must be some element of causation. For example, if the defendant was able to sell more widgets because it had greater manufacturing capacity than the plaintiff patentee, not all profits from sale of defendant's infringing widgets would be appropriate.

231. **The best answer is D**. All the other factors are among the many considered by the Federal Circuit in evaluating the egregiousness of the defendant's conduct.

232. **The best answer is B**. Willful infringement may establish a basis for enhanced damages. Answer A is incorrect because a court has discretion to determine whether or not to impose enhanced damages. **Answers C and D are incorrect** because they state inferences that the Federal Circuit has overruled in *Knorr-Bremse v. Dana Corp* to better accommodate the prior tension with attorney-client privilege.

233. **The best answer is B**. Generally, all products made by a patentee must be marked not only with the word "patent" or "pat," but also with the actual patent number. **Answer D is incorrect** because it fails to mention the patent number. **C is incorrect** because there is no exception from the marking rule for patents that were first published as applications. However, one exception from the regular rule for patent marking is that processes need not be patented. **Answer A is incorrect** because it is overbroad. Failure to mark a patented product will limit recovery, but the patentee is not completely barred from all relief. Rather, the patentee can only claim damages from the date the accused infringer first had actual notice of patent infringement, such as by being served with a complaint for patent infringement.

234. If the infringer is the federal government, the only remedy is a suit for "reasonable and entire compensation" in the Court of Federal Claims under 28 U.S.C. 1498. There is no possibility of obtaining an injunction against the infringement.

235. **Answer D is the best answer. Answer C is incorrect** because although it is always possible to obtain monetary damages for infringement after patent issuances, in *some* cases it is also possible to obtain damages for activity within the scope of the claims of a published patent application. In particular, if the scope of the final claims are "substantially identical" to those in the published patent application and the defendant had actual notice of the published application, the defendant could be liable for "provisional rights" under 35 U.S.C. 154(d) **Answers A and B are incorrect**, however, since no damages are appropriate before the application is published.

PRACTICE FINAL EXAM: ANSWERS

236. **The best answer is A.** Naturally occurring biological material is not patentable, such that **Answer B is incorrect** for being over-inclusive. Answer A presents the best option by clarifying that while naturally occurring plants are not patentable, a genetically modified plant would be. On the other hand, Answer B falsely asserts that genes in their natural state are patentable. Only isolated genes constitute patentable subject matter. In addition, although not an issue here, patentability may be impeded by other criteria, such as novelty and nonboviousness. **Answer C is incorrect** because there is no exclusion from patentability for methods of performing medicine. While there may be a policy argument that patents should not be granted for methods of performing surgery, Congress has elected to address this issue by making the methods patentable, but not enforceable against doctors who might infringe (under 35 U.S.C 287(c)). However, the patent is still potentially enforceable against those who contribute to the direct infringement by doctors. **Answer D is incorrect** because it confuses the concepts of patentable subject matter and utility. A new game may be patentable subject matter as a method of entertainment. In addition, although utility is subject of a different section, utility as entertainment is also acceptable.

237. **The best answer is C** since 102(f) is the only provision here that would be relevant. To be rejected based upon 102(a) or (b) there must be published prior art, or prior art within the United States. There is no such prior art here — knowledge known outside the United States does not qualify, so **Answers A and B are incorrect**. On the other hand, derivation under 102(f) may be established without regard to the place from which it was derived. The only important element is that the invention was previously conceived by another, as corroborated through testimony and/or documentation. Since only 102(f) works, **Answer D is also incorrect**.

238. **The best answer is D**. Every patent claim stands alone in terms of assessing infringement. Accordingly, a defendant may be liable even if he only infringes a single claim of a multi-claim patent. The number of claims infringed is relevant to damages. **Answer A is incorrect** because direct infringement is not synonymous with literal infringement. Rather, direct infringement can exist if the defendant infringements every element of a claim either literally or via the doctrine of equivalents. **Answer B is incorrect** because there is no requirement that a patent owner make his own invention as a pre-requisite

163

for asserting infringement. **Answer C is incorrect** because while direct infringement is a pre-requisite for contributory infringement, the direct infringer need not be an official legal party for contributory infringement claim to survive.

239. **The best answer is C. Answer A is incorrect** because the application itself must satisfy the requirements of 112, including enablement. **Answer B is incorrect** because any changes to the application would constitute improper new matter. **Answer D is also incorrect** because references to material outside the application must exist at the time the application is originally filed to satisfy 112. Although a continuation in patent application is undesirable with respect to the fact that the new material is only entitled to the new filing date, it is the only possible option to obtain a valid patent that complies with 112.

240. **The best answer is D. Answer B is incorrect** because the U.S. provides patents based upon a "first to invent" philosophy, rather than a "first to file" philosophy. **Answer A is incorrect** because an invention can only be anticipated by prior art. The fact that Javier reduced the invention to practice does not alone constitute prior art. In addition, although sales of an invention can constitute public use or knowledge, such prior art is limited to activity within the United States; accordingly, no activity by Javier here is relevant to 102(a). The fact that Peru is a WTO country is a red herring since a country's WTO status is not relevant to 102(a); it may be relevant to establishing the date of an invention in an interference under 102(g), but no answers here address whether there is an interference. **Answer C is incorrect** because the U.S. does not recognize prior use rights except for the limited class of business method patents. Independent invention is not a defense to patent infringement (although it is to copyright infringement).

241. The issue here is whether the paper, a printed publication, would bar Lisa's patent under 102(a). Based on Lisa's filing date of October 1, 2007, the USPTO would likely reject her application under 102(a). However, she can file a 1.131 affidavit to establish that she reduced the invention to practice on March 30, 2007, narrowly avoiding the April 1, 2007 prior art.

242. **The best answer is C. Answer A is incorrect** because the United States does not permit third parties to oppose patent applications. **Answer B is incorrect** because an applicant can only claim an earlier filing date from an application made by the same applicant. **Answer D is incorrect** because an interference proceeding requires that there be at least one patent application such that the USPTO has jurisdiction. If both Javier and Lisa had issued patents, there would be no basis to declare an interference.

243. **The best answer is C. Answer D is incorrect** because a bar to patentability under 102(g)(2) only exists if before the applicant's invention the same invention was made in the United States by someone who did not abandon, suppress, or conceal it. Although 102(g) does permit activity outside the United States to be considered, it is only for the purposes of interferences under 102(g)(1) and only for NAFTA and WTO countries.

Answers A and B are incorrect because 102(b) is based upon prior art that takes place more than one year before the date of application; the date of the applicant's actual conception or reduction to practice is not relevant for 102(b). Invention dates are relevant for 102(a) and 102(g), but not 102(b).

244. **The best answer is D** since a patent owner's status as a non-manufacturing patent owner may be considered, although not necessarily a dispositive factor, by courts in considering whether to grant injunctive relief since injunction is an equitable remedy. In addition, a prevailing patent owner is always entitled to at least a reasonable royalty by statute. Accordingly, **Answer A and B are incorrect**. In addition, Answer A is also incorrect because there is no absolute bar based upon whether the owner of a patent is a non-manufacturing patentee. **Answer C is incorrect** because although the patentee's status as a non-manufacturing patent owner is considered, there is no absolute bar to recovery.

245. **The best answer is D**. A patent owner has the right to exclude all others from making, using, selling, offering to sell, or importing the patented invention. All of the situations described in choices A-C involve importing the patented invention, such that **Answers A–C are incorrect**. A patent may be infringed when the claimed device is imported, even if it was first purchased in a location where it was unpatented. The fact that the device was not patented in Ireland simply means that it can be made, used, and sold in Ireland without liability; it does not mean that it can be freely imported into the U.S. Answers B and C are slightly more complicated since they involve the doctrine of exhaustion. The general rule of exhaustion, otherwise known as first sale, is that the first sale within the United States of the patented invention exhausts the patent owner's rights with respect to that specific item. The owner of the physical product can thereafter convey the item as he or she wishes. However, whether the sale of the patent owner's product outside the United States exhausts the patent owner's rights within the United States involves the doctrine of international exhaustion. The Federal Circuit has held that authorized sales abroad do not exhaust the patent owner's rights at the U.S. border. Accordingly, the importation from Mexico and Japan both constitute infringement, even though they bought products from the patent owner, or an authorized dealer.

246. **Answer D is the best answer.** Best mode is determined based upon a two-part inquiry, the first part of which considers whether the inventor had a best mode. If so, the second issue is an objective analysis of whether the inventor actually disclosed her best mode in the application. Even though the second step involves an element of objectivity, the focus is still on the inventor's perceived best mode. Accordingly, it is irrelevant if there is objectively a better mode not known to the inventor. In addition, enablement is satisfied if a person of skill in the art would be able to make and use the claimed invention based upon the specification without undue experimentation. This can be satisfied even if not every member of the class is disclosed where all members of the class actually work as intended. On the other hand, if someone of skill in the art would have to engage in undue experimentation to figure out which of the claimed class actually had the claimed conductivity, enablement would not be satisfied. Because both best

mode and enablement exist, **Answers A-C are incorrect**, since they all suggest that at least one of these requirements does not exist.

247. **The best answer is D.** Literal infringement can only exist if the defendant's device falls within all elements of the patented invention. The question expressly states that does not happen here. In addition, infringement under the doctrine of equivalents requires more than similarity of the overall product, such that **Answer A is incorrect**. In particular, the accused product must satisfy every element of the claimed invention either literally or under the doctrine of equivalents. Since there is no information that this exists here, B is not liable. **Answer B is incorrect** since secondary infringement requires direct infringement by someone and none appears in the question. **C is incorrect** because although B could arguably be considered to have derived the general idea for his yo-yo from A's patent, derivation is only an issue with respect to patentability for B. Derivation is not an affirmative cause of action.

248. **The best answer is D.** Knackoff does not infringe under 271(a) because direct infringement requires that all claimed elements are satisfied. Here, because the claim requires the dispenser to be assembled, Knackoff cannot infringe. Knackoff may be liable for secondary infringement under 271(b) for inducing infringement. However, liability will only exist if Knackoff knew of the patent and someone actually infringes. If no one buys the kits, Knackoff cannot be liable since secondary infringement can never exist without direct infringement by someone. **Answer A is incorrect** because liability under 271(a) only exists if the entire claimed invention is made, used, offered for sale, sold, or imported. "Substantially all" of the claimed invention, even if it is very close, is inadequate. Also, the doctrine of equivalents also does not suffice because that only helps where an accused product has an equivalent to an element of the claimed invention. It does not cover the situation where most, but not all, of the claimed invention is made and there is no issue of equivalent elements of the claimed invention. **Answer B is incorrect** because infringement under 271(a) can exist for either selling or offering to sell the claimed invention. So, even if no one accepts an offer for sale, liability can still ensue if the claimed invention is on sale. However, in this case, since the claimed assembly is not actually on sale, there is no infringement. **Answer C is incorrect** because liability under 271(f) is premised on supplying the components of the patented invention for assembly abroad. There is nothing in the facts here to suggest that the kits are actually assembled abroad, or that there is even any intent for such assembly to occur abroad.

249. **The best answer is D.** Inducement requires that someone directly infringe. In addition, the direct infringement must have been induced by Knackoff based on actual knowledge of the patent, together with actions intended to induce the infringement. **Answer A is incorrect** because inducement cannot exist without knowledge of the patent. Mere intent to induce actions that happen to cause infringement without knowledge of the patent is inadequate. **Answer B is incorrect** because inducement, like all secondary infringement, may never exist without direct infringement by someone. **Answer C is incorrect** because it confuses the elements of 271(b) (contributory infringement) with 271(c) (inducement). In particular, inducement is not concerned with staple products or whether

components have substantial non-infringing uses — these are only relevant to contributory infringement where one a component that is a material part of the invention is sold or offered for sale. Although Knockoff possibly also could be liable for contributory infringement, that is not relevant to this question since the question asked solely about inducement.

250. **The best answer is D.** The ability to enjoin infringing users depends first on a patent claim being infringed. Infringement, in turn, depends first on the construction of the claims. If Bob's patent claim is limited to only some types of French toast or only toast made by a particular method that would substantially limit who Bob can enforce his patent against. Accordingly, **Answer A is incorrect** since it is overbroad. **C is incorrect** because patent infringement does not depend on knowledge of a patent. There is one limited exception for business method patents, but that is not at issue here. **Answer B is incorrect** both because the scope of Bob's patent claim is presently unclear. In addition, the doctrine of equivalents is only relevant to substitute elements of a claim and not for the entire product. Moreover, the patent here appears to be for a method, so only a method can infringe — not the product produced by a method.

251. **The best answer is A.** The issue here is whether Sally's compound is a species of a broader genus that was previously disclosed in the prior art. Sally's date of invention is October 1, 2007 (constructive reduction to practice) since the facts state that she has not actually reduced to practice before this time. As of that date, Mitch's application constitutes prior art as a printed publication made available on September 15, 2007. Mitch's application discloses the genus that includes Sally's invention, so she is barred under 102(a). **Answer B is incorrect** because it fails to recognize that Sally's invention is barred by 102(a). There is no need to consider 102(e) when there is patent-defeating prior art that exists at the time of the applicant's invention. **Answers C and D are incorrect** because a claimed invention is barred by prior art that describes all elements of the claimed invention. It is not necessary or relevant that the prior art claims the identical invention unless the issue is 102(g). In addition, choices C and D are incorrect since Sally's invention is anticipated; there is no need to consider obviousness. Answer D is also incorrect because common assignment under 103(c) is only relevant where the prior art is solely based on 102(e), (f), or (g). Here, where the relevant prior art is 102(a), this provision would not be relevant.

252. **The best answer is B.** Mitch's application is relevant prior art under 102(e) as a prior U.S. application that is now published. It is irrelevant that Walt had no actual knowledge of Mitch's application, or even that Walt could not have known about Mitch's then-secret application. **Answer A is incorrect** because 102(e) is generally not publicly available. The "publicly available" talisman is relevant to prior art under 102(a) and (b), but not 102(e); indeed, 102(e) art is often called "secret" prior art. **Answer D is incorrect** because to claim the benefit of an earlier filing date, you need not only co-pending applications, but at least one inventor in common. Here, there are no inventors in common. Being part of a common endeavor, such as a joint research agreement, is not sufficient. **Answer C is incorrect** because it misstates the test for when prior art that

would typically be used for obviousness analyses are statutorily excluded under 103(c). In particular, for prior art based on 102(e), (f), or (g) may not bar patentability if the prior art and the claimed invention were owned by the same person or subject to assignment to the same person. However, the statute defines the ownership or assignment provision to include inventions that are made as a result of joint research agreements under 103(c)(2).

253.   **The best answer is C.** Inequitable conduct renders the patent completely unenforceable — both in the existing case and in future cases. **Answer A is incorrect** because the validity of each claim is considered separately. Pursuant to 35 U.S.C 282, dependent claims are presumed valid, even if they depend upon an invalid claim. Essentially, if the independent claim is found invalid, the dependent claim is simply deemed to incorporate all the elements of the now invalid independent claim and evaluated on its own as if it were originally written as an independent claim. **Answer B is incorrect** because issue preclusion, otherwise known as collateral estoppel, bars the owner of an adjudicated invalid patent from asserting the validity of the patent against a different accused infringer — so long as the patentee had a full and fair opportunity to litigate the validity issue in the original proceeding. If the patentee attempts to assert the patent against the new party, the new party can raise collateral estoppel as an affirmative defense. **Answer D is incorrect** because actual knowledge is never relevant to assessing direct infringement. In addition, there is no defense based upon prior independent invention.

254.   **The best answer is B.** Direct infringement exists if the defendant makes, sells, offers to sell, or imports the claimed invention. Importation is one of the prohibited activities under 271(a). Accordingly, even though she did not infringe by making the claimed invention within the United States, **Answer A is incorrect** because that is not the only potential basis for liability. Similarly, although sales and offers to sell are bases for establishing infringement, any of the listed activities under 271(a) are sufficient; so the fact that she has not yet sold or offered for sale the invention does not automatically immunize her from infringement, making **Answer D incorrect**. In addition, in assessing whether the accused device has all elements of the claimed invention, every element must exist either literally or under the doctrine of equivalents. **Answer C is incorrect** because infringement is evaluated separate and apart from whether a defendant has its own patent. It is possible for a defendant to infringe and yet have a patent on an improved product or process. The only relevant inquiry for infringement is whether the accused device has all the elements of the claimed invention.

255.   **Answer D is the best answer.** The issue here is the relevance of whether equivalents were unknown at the time the claimed invention was filed. For doctrine of equivalents, infringement may exist even if the equivalents were unknown at the time of the invention. However, for infringement of a 112, paragraph 6 claim, the claim is interpreted to be based upon what is specifically disclosed in the specifications and equivalents to what is disclosed known at the time of the invention. In other words, means plus function claims cannot cover after-arising equivalents. **Answer A is**

incorrect because infringement under the doctrine of equivalents is not limited to what was known at the time of the invention. **Answer B is incorrect** because even if Leah's invention is new, that does not bar an infringement claim. **Answer C is incorrect** because any claim that is a means plus function claim can only use equivalents that are known at the time of the invention.

256. **The best answer is D.** Although commercial success and licensing activity may be relevant considerations in an obviousness analysis, the key inquiry is whether the secondary factors have a nexus to the claimed invention, such that the success is likely due to the invention being a substantial improvement over the prior art. The fact that she has no prior sales experience that could weigh in her favor since her commercial success would not be based on market dominance. However, there is no indication that the level of activity is because of the Lipton-based spaceships, as opposed to the success of her marketing campaign. High commercial volume is not equivalent to commercial success based upon the properties of the claimed invention. So, Answer B is incorrect. **Answer C is also incorrect** because an invention can be nonobvious without having a majority of the nonobviousness factors in favor of the invention. Rather, the evaluation is a holistic one and there is no absolute number of elements that must be satisfied. **Answer A is incorrect** because disclaiming Kypton would not be enough to rebut a claim of obviousness. If Leah had a claim that encompassed Kypton as well as other compounds, such that there was an anticipation problem, specifically disclaiming Kypton would be helpful. However, for an obviousness rejection, she must also show that her invention is not obvious in light of Luke's patent.

257. **The best answer is C.** An analysis of obviousness must be based upon only analogous art. Analogous prior art is either prior art from the same endeavor, or prior art from a different endeavor that would nonetheless have been pertinent to the problem being solved by a person of ordinary skill. The first question is what constitutes the field of endeavor? Is it directed only to containers for holding coffee, or any container for holding and pouring beverages? Since the claims are not limited to coffee, but, rather, claim any liquid container, considering any prior art regarding liquid containers seems relevant. In addition, even if the endeavor was interpreted narrowly, the "problem being solved" would likely encompass the prior wine container in terms of a means for storing and pouring the liquid. **Answer A is incorrect** because the claimed invention does not mention center of gravity. Even if the specification discusses this as an advantage, since the focus of the analysis is the claimed invention, the lack of any such mention makes it irrelevant. In addition, even if the claims had included something about center of gravity, it is still questionable whether the golf club would be considered pertinent prior art. While the golf club may mention center of gravity, only a very broad consideration of the problem being solved would include the golf club. In particular, the invention here is not merely about creating something with a center of gravity; the function of the invention as something that can contain and pour liquid is also important. **Answer B is incorrect** because actual knowledge is never relevant for something to be considered as prior art. The relevant consideration for whether something is relevant art under 103 is whether it would have been considered relevant to a person of ordinary skill in the

art. **Answer D is incorrect** because patent-defeating public use is not limited to use by the patentee or patent applicant.

258. **The best answer is D.** Although a patent is presumed valid and a court would certainly undertake the re-examination procedure, the court is not estopped from making its own independent assessment, including an opposite result. The only limitation on the court is to make sure that obviousness is shown by clear and convincing evidence. **Answer A is incorrect** because any reference may be considered in challenging a patent in litigation; there is no requirement that the reference be first considered by the PTO. **Answer B is incorrect** because analysis under 103 does not require complete identity; a single reference with all the claimed elements is only necessary for 102(a) anticipation. If the wine container is being used in an obviousness analysis for the over frame and spout, but the claimed handle is provided from a different reference, that is appropriate for 103 analysis. **Answer C is incorrect** because it states the false standard for establishing obviousness. In particular, obviousness must be established by clear and convincing evidence. However there is no need to prove obviousness beyond a reasonable doubt.

259. **The best answer is A.** The term of a patent is calculated from the effective filing date. Here, the effective filing date would be the date of the provisional application from which the nonprovisional depends. In addition, the patent term is 20 years from the earliest filing date, or, twenty years from February 15, 2006. **Answer B is incorrect** because it uses the date of the nonprovisional application. **Answers C and D are incorrect** because they are based on the issuance date. In addition, **Answer D is incorrect** in using a period of seventeen years. Although patent terms were at one point calculated as seventeen years from date of issuance, that is not the case for presently issued patents.

260. **The best answer is B.** For a CIP application, there are different dates used for examining prior art, depending on which application supports the claims. For claims that are supported by the earlier specification, section 120 is satisfied and the earlier filing date can be used. On the other hand, for claims that are supported only by the later CIP application, the later filing date must be used. Because the priority date depends on which application supports the claims, **Answer C is incorrect** — not all the claims can be supported by the initial application. Similarly, **Answer D is also incorrect** because some claims are supported by the earlier date, such that they are entitled to use the earlier filing date. **Answer A is incorrect** because while it is true that no new matter may be added to applications as a general matter, a CIP by definition adds new matter to the previous application. There is no violation here though since claims supported by the new matter are examined based upon the later date.

261. **The best answer is C.** For most patents, the term is 20 years from the filing date. For a CIP, there are different terms for different patent claims since they do not all use the same date of invention. Answer C is the only choice to accurately describe the differing terms. **Answer A is incorrect** because it uses the earlier date for all claims,

including ones that are not supported by the earlier application. **Answer B is incorrect** because it is based on the date of filing for the CIP, but some claims are entitled to an earlier filing date. **Answer D is incorrect** because it calculates the term from date of patent issuance and not from date of filing. In addition, the date of publication of the application was a red herring, although it was not specifically referred to in the answers.

262. **The best answer is C.** The first issue here is whether infringement can occur in a claim to a physical structure, even if the use is different than the one described in the specification. Because the claims are directed only at the physical structure, a court would likely construe the claims to cover any device with the same physical structure, so **Answer B is incorrect**. While it is true that claims are construed in light of the specification and the specification focuses on detangling pets, unless the specification stated that it could only work on pets, there would not seem to be any need to so limit the claims. In addition, the relatively simple nature of the invention would suggest that someone of skill in the art would read the specification and know that other uses of the brush other than the ones disclosed were possible. **Answer A is incorrect**, although a good second choice, because a complete defense to infringement is the doctrine of first sale. In particular, even if the cleaning company is using the claimed invention, the patent owner, Barry, cannot assert a claim against the company if the company bought the brush from an authorized dealer. The first authorized sale of a patented invention within the United States exhausts the patent owner's rights in that object. If, on the other hand, the cleaning company made additional brushes on its own, it would be liable for infringement. **Answer D is incorrect** because it misstates the damages limitations period under 35 U.S.C 286. If a patent owner waits more than six years from knowledge of infringement to bring a litigation suit, the patent owner is barred from recovering damages for the six years prior to the initiation of the litigation. However, Barry can still obtain damages that accrue after litigation is initiated, as well as a possible injunction.

263. **The best answer is D.** The first issue is that a legal purchaser (from the patentee or an authorized dealer) of a patented device has an implied license to use the device, including a right to repair it. The major issue here is whether fixing the bristles constitutes permissible repair or impermissible (and thus infringing) reconstruction. Although it is often difficult to distinguish between permitted repair versus prohibited reconstruction, heating the brush and adding additional material seems more like reconstruction of the claimed invention. Also, whether the part being "fixed" would be expected to be spent is another relevant fact. This fact pattern is based upon *Sandvik v. EJ*, in which the Federal Circuit found that the defendant's retipping of drills constituted infringing reconstruction because the drills were "spent" before retipping and the retipping involved re-melting the tips and reshaping them. **Answer B is incorrect** because reconstruction can exist even if only part of the patented invention is subject to fixing. **Answer C is incorrect** because liability can exist without specific claims to the brushes. **Answer A is incorrect** because, as noted above, an authorized purchase is only the first issue to consider.

264.   **The best answer is B**. The facts state that there is no prior art before her invention, so her car is not anticipated under 102(a). Accordingly, **Answer A is incorrect**. The key issue here is whether the activity on the blog is patent-defeating under 102(b). First, the blog entry occurred more than one year before the date of application, so the timing is appropriate for 102(b). So, the next question is whether the blog entry qualifies as a printed publication. Such a publication must be sufficiently accessible to the relevant public. Although the blog entry is not a formal publication, that is not necessary; a blog entry on the Internet is sufficiently accessible to the relevant public. So, **Answer D is incorrect**. In addition, it does not matter for purposes of 102(b) that she wrote the entry herself — 102(b) bars patentability based on the activity of anyone, including the inventor. So, **Answer C is incorrect**.

265.   **The best answer is D**. The relevant prior art here is a publication. **Answers B and C are incorrect** because experimental use is not relevant where the 102(b) bar is based upon the applicant's prior publication. Experimental use can negate what would otherwise constitute public use or an invention that is "on sale." However, it is not applicable to all prior art under 102(b). **Answer A is also incorrect** because the focus of 102(b) is not on whether the invention was novel, but whether the applicant is statutorily barred because of undue delay in seeking an invention.

266.   **The best answer is C**. A prior U.S. application can be a bar under 102(e) even if the applicant could not have known about the prior application as an unpublished application at the time. So long as Kitty's patent application is published, it qualifies as prior art under 102(e). It is not necessary for the application to be published before George files and in fact most likely would not since prior art under this provision is usually referred to as "secret prior art" since it typically is not public at the time the applicant files an application. **Answer A is incorrect** because there is no 102(a) prior art before George's invention. Although Kitty may have previously conceived and reduced to practice, any use by Kitty occurred outside the United States and thus does not qualify as 102(a) prior art. **Answer B is incorrect** because 102(d) only applies if the invention is first patented by the applicant. There is no prior patent here. In addition, the prior application is by Kitty and not George. Section 102(d) is intended to promote prompt filing of U.S. applications claiming priority from foreign applications, but that does not apply to this case. **Answer D is incorrect** because 102(g)(2) only applies if Kitty had made the invention in this country before George. Because Kitty made the invention outside the United States, that would not be a bar under this provision.

267.   **The best answer is C**. For either a reissue or a re-examination proceeding, the original patent must be surrendered before the patent is examined. Although a patent often issues, a reissue proceeding may result in complete loss of a patent, thus making the proceeding somewhat risky. **Answer D is incorrect** because reexamination proceedings may only be granted based upon a substantial new question of patentability, defined as questions concerning prior art. A number of patentability requirements are beyond the scope of re-examination, such as patentable subject matter, Section 112, and inventorship. **Answer B is incorrect** because re-examinations may be sought at any time, but are

limited to two years only if there is a request to broaden any aspect of the patent. **Answer A is incorrect** because while anyone may seek reexamination, reissue may only be requested by the patentee.

268. **The best answer is A**. The key claim term here is "consisting," which limits infringement to products that contain exactly and only elements A, B, and C. In addition, **Answers B, C, and D are incorrect** because they all have an additional element. Whether or not Elaine has a patent is a red herring: whether a defendant has a patent is never relevant to whether the defendant infringes.

269. **The best answer is D**. The key here is that the claim contains the word "comprising," such that infringement exists for any widget that has at least the elements A, B, and C. In addition, selling the patented invention (widgets comprising at least A+B+C) is also an activity that gives rise to infringement. **Answer A is incorrect** because Elaine sells widgets that do not have all the elements of the patented invention. **Answers B and C are incorrect** because they contain red herrings concerning a possible infringement by doctrine of equivalents. While the doctrine may be utilized to find infringement of an element that is not met literally, the doctrine requires looking to whether there is an insubstantial difference between the element of the patented invention versus the accused invention. The analysis is not based on the overall product. Moreover, although one way to assess insubstantial difference is the tripartite test, this test requires that the infringing element in the accused product do so with the same function, way, and result as the claimed element.

270. **The best answer is C**. The French patent application does not constitute prior art because it was not published prior to the U.S. application. The fact that the French application was published after the U.S. application was filed is irrelevant. Although prior applications can sometimes constitute prior art when a later application is issued, that is only relevant when the prior application was a prior U.S. application, or a prior international application filed in English, according to 102(e). Answer A focuses on a relevant issue for evaluating whether an invention is entitled to an earlier filing date, but **Answer A is incorrect** because the reference may be added anytime during prosecution of the U.S. application. **Answer B is incorrect**, even though it makes an accurate statement because it is not the best answer. Answer C is similar, but more complete. **Answer D is incorrect** because the relevant inquiry for 119 purposes is simply whether the same invention was disclosed and not whether the same invention was claimed.

271. **The best answer is A.** This question is a bit tricky since it raises issue of foreign priority under Section 119 where there are two different foreign filings prior to the U.S. application. Under Section 119, an applicant can claim the benefit of the earlier foreign filing date if the applicant (or his legal representatives or assignees) has previously filed an application for the same invention in a foreign country. In other words, even though the actual U.S. filing date is later, the applicant gets the earlier (foreign filing) date for purposes of comparing the U.S. claims to prior art. To get the benefit of the earlier

date, the earlier foreign application must provide a written description of the claimed U.S. invention, as well as an enabling disclosure of the claimed U.S. invention and a best mode (if one exists). Essentially, the foreign application must satisfy all of the Section 112 ¶ 1 requirements for the applicant to rely on its filing date.

The key issue to answering this question is knowing that the benefit of an earlier filing date under Section 119 only works if the U.S. application is filed within one year of the earliest date on which a foreign application was filed — the inventor cannot use the last foreign filing date. **Answer B is incorrect**. Although the Hungarian application date is not over a year from the date of the French application, this is of no help to Hank if he cannot get the benefit of the French application date. As noted above, he cannot do so here because Section 119 only allows an applicant to claim the benefit of an earlier date when the U.S. application is filed twelve months from the earliest foreign application. **Answer C is incorrect** because Hank cannot claim the benefit of an earlier filing date under 119 since he filed the U.S. application more than 12 months after the earliest filing date. There is no basis for Hank to claim February 1, 2004 as an effective date. The earliest actual date that Hank filed on any application was February 1, 2005, and he cannot use this date, let alone an arbitrary date one year earlier. **Answer D is wrong** because a foreign application only bars a U.S. application if the foreign application issues as an actual patent. Since the facts here specifically state that the Hungarian application was published but not granted, there is no 102(d) bar. Hank is out of luck, but not because of 102(d).

Although this question did not attempt to test the nuances of what foreign filings would not apply, the rule is that the benefit of an earlier foreign filing date is only applicable for applications filed in foreign countries which provide similar privileges for previously filed U.S. applications, or U.S. citizens, as well as any WTO member country. Given that the scope of the WTO is nearly 200 countries, including both major countries and relatively small ones, most foreign countries are included. Both Hungary and France are WTO countries.

272. **The best answer is B**. Where an applicant claims the benefit of an earlier priority date, that date is used both for prior art purposes, as well as calculating the patent term. Answer B is the date of the earlier foreign application. **Answers A and D are incorrect** because the patent term is not based upon the date of issuance of the patent for applications filed since 1996. In addition, **Answer C is incorrect** since the earlier priority date is used for the patent term, even if the earlier application was not filed in the United States.

273. **The best answer is C**. When a reissue application is requested, the patent owner must surrender the actual patent; accordingly, there is no patent that is enforceable unless and until the patent is reissued. **Answer B is incorrect** because reissue applications are appropriate both when a patentee seeks to narrow or broaden claims, so long as the patent is wholly or partially invalid and the error is without any deceptive intent on the part of the patent owner. Although there is a two-year limit on filing reissue

applications when a patentee seeks to broaden claims that should not be confused with limiting reissue applications to narrowed claims only. **Answer A is incorrect** since the statutory presumption of validity is the same for all patents. There is no enhanced statutory presumption of validity. While a jury may make its own presumptions based upon the fact that the USPTO has examined the patent twice, this is not the best answer. **Answer D is incorrect** because spelling errors in the name of the inventor would not be grounds for a reissue application. In particular, the patent would not be wholly or partly inoperative or invalid. However, the patent could be corrected by filing a certificate of correction so long as the error arose without deceptive intent.

274. **The best answer is B. Answer A is close, but not the best answer** because it is not the most complete answer. Answer A correctly notes that Donald does not infringe since he bought the patented product from a licensed manufacturer. Thus, Donald was using the patented invention without infringement. This may also be construed as the "first sale" doctrine in that the first sale of a patented item exhausts the patentee's rights in that item.

Answer C is incorrect because it misstates Donald's liability, as well as Donald's ability to obtain his own patent. Although Donald will be barred from obtaining a patent on the same composition, he may nonetheless obtain a patent for a new method as long as that method is nonobvious. **Answer D is incorrect** not only because it misstates Donald's liability, but also because utility is satisfied if a patent establishes a single utility. Claudia's patent does so here. In addition, even if Claudia did not discover S's utility as a method for treating baldness, Claudia's patent on the composition is valid against anyone who makes X for such purpose. This example illustrates why composition patents are more valuable than method patents.

275. **The best answer is C.** Theresa cannot obtain a patent claiming the melatonin composition because that would be anticipated by the prior art. Even if there is no disclosure in the prior art concerning the use of melatonin for this new purpose, she is still barred from obtaining a claim to the product itself. For anticipation purposes, prior art need not disclose the claimed use; this is an important distinction from what the specification of a claimed invention must disclose (both how to make and use the claimed invention). Accordingly, **Answer D is inaccurate** since no claim to melatonin composition is possible. However, she can obtain a patent on a new use of an existing product; the prior art only discloses the composition and not the use. This shows one distinction between claiming a product versus a method. Although a product claim is broader and provides more protection, if the product is previously known in the prior art — even for a different use — such a claim will be precluded.

Answer A is not the best answer in light of the other options. While it is true that Theresa did make observations, not every invention needs to involve the concoction of materials. Moreover, method patents typically involve experimentation with old compounds. Whether or not something rises to the level of a patentable invention should probably be determined based upon whether it satisfies the other statutory criteria, such as novelty. **Answer B is incorrect** because it is less complete than Answer C. As noted above, any attempt to claim melatonin would be anticipated by the prior art, but her intention is not to patent the composition itself.

276. The issue here is whether the prior movie (a printed publication?) would constitute anticipatory prior art. This is unlikely since the prior art would need to disclose every element of the claimed invention. A person of ordinary skill in the art would likely not find all elements of the claimed invention in the movie. Indeed, the car in the movie likely was not operable and an anticipatory piece of prior art must provide sufficient disclosure to enable someone of skill in the art to make the claimed invention. Considering that time travel is of interest to some, but no one has made a time travel machine with the flux capacitor in the movie since that time, this is unlikely.

277. **The best answer is D** since none of the other choices state a reason why the patent would be invalid. Enablement is satisfied if the specification enables someone of skill in the art to make and use the claimed invention. Here, the claim is to a chemical composition and not to the best-ever treatment for arthritis. Since the facts state that specification discloses how to make and use the composition in detail, enablement is satisfied, such that **Answer A is incorrect**. Similarly, best mode is satisfied if the inventor's best mode of practicing the invention at the time of application is disclosed. Here, the hair growth discovery occurred after application and there is no requirement to update best mode (moreover, modifying the specification would constitute impermissible new matter), so **Answer B is also incorrect**. **Answer C is also wrong**, since utility is satisfied so long as one substantial and credible utility is disclosed. To satisfy utility, the specification need not disclose a more efficacious compound. In particular, whether the FDA would deem the compound useful, let alone clinically superior, that is irrelevant for patent purposes. So long as the utility is credible and not a "throwaway" utility that could be asserted with every invention, it is likely credible.

278. **The best answer is A**. Direct infringement exists whenever someone makes the claimed invention and there is no defense to such infringement. Here, the facts state that Jack and Jill made the claimed composition covered by the Zano patent. The issue covered by Answers B and C is whether their use can be immunized based on an experimental use defense. The statutory experimental use defense is a very narrow one intended for researchers who are experimenting on compounds for the purpose of FDA approval, but no facts are provided to suggest that they were engaged in any such use. Technically, there is also a common law experimental use defense, but this defense is very narrow and generally only covers use done for idle curiosity. Given the fact that they were making the composition during the course of a specific research activity, the creation was not idle curiosity; therefore, **Answer B is incorrect**. **Answer D is also incorrect** because while Jack and Jill are first to discover the use of the compound for treating hepatitis, a valid patent only needs to disclose a single use. Jack and Jill may be entitled to a method of use patent, but they are still liable for direct infringement if Zano elects to pursue such a claim against them. Their only hope of avoiding liability based on these facts would be if Zano does not bring suit.

279. **The best answer is B.** Judy cannot obtain a patent on a naturally occurring product, regardless of whether she is the first to "discover" it, since this is not patentable subject matter, making **Answer A incorrect. Answer C is incorrect** because while it accurately states that no patent is possible on the natural plant, it inaccurately states that a patent is not possible based upon a purified version. Isolated and purified versions of natural compounds are patentable if they are nonobvious and there is no absolute bar to their patentability. **Answer D is incorrect**, albeit the second-best answer, in that it recognizes Judy could patent the purified version. Although Judy may be the first to seek a patent on a method of using natural Ocam, she derived this knowledge from another, so that the method would be barred under 102(f).

280. **The best answer is C.** There is no anticipation under 102(a) because there is no prior art before Jill's application that disclosed every element of the claimed invention. Indeed, it appears that Jill was the first to make a synthetic variant. The natural Ocam cannot anticipate under 102(a) since Jill is not claiming the natural form. Also, if Jill had claimed the natural form, that would not be patentable because natural compounds do not constitute patentable subject matter. Although there is no prior art in the U.S., the invention may be obvious based upon 102(f) and 103. Unlike other categories of prior art, 102(f) is not geographically limited. If a synthetic variant of what Jill was shown would be obvious, that could bar patentability. **Answer D is incorrect** because it fails to recognize a Section 103 problem. **Answer A is incorrect** because public use must be use in the U.S. and there was no such use. In addition, any public use was of the natural Ocam and not the synthetic variant. **Answer B is incorrect** because the natural Ocam does not anticipate all elements of the synthetic Ocam — while the two may have similar properties, the claim is unlikely to cover the natural variety.

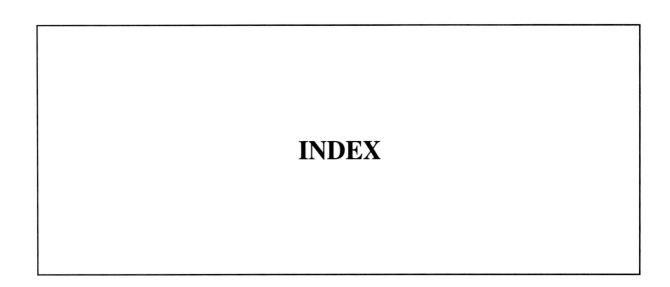

INDEX

INDEX

TOPIC   **QUESTION**

DOCTRINE OF EQUIVALENTS

EFFECTIVE FILING DATE